AMERICAN EDUCATION

Its Men

Ideas

and

Institutions

Advisory Editor

Lawrence A. Cremin
Frederick A. P. Barnard Professor of Education
Teachers College, Columbia University

The Selective Character of American Secondary Education

George S. Counts

ARNO PRESS & THE NEW YORK TIMES

*New York * 1969*

Reprint edition 1969 by Arno Press, Inc.

*

Library of Congress Catalog Card No. 75-89166

*

Reprinted from a copy in Teachers College Library

*

Manufactured in the United States of America

Editorial Note

AMERICAN EDUCATION: *Its Men, Institutions and Ideas* presents selected works of thought and scholarship that have long been out of print or otherwise unavailable. Inevitably, such works will include particular ideas and doctrines that have been outmoded or superseded by more recent research. Nevertheless, all retain their place in the literature, having influenced educational thought and practice in their own time and having provided the basis for subsequent scholarship.

Lawrence A. Cremin
Teachers College

The Selective Character of
American Secondary Education

SUPPLEMENTARY EDUCATIONAL MONOGRAPHS

Published in conjunction with

THE SCHOOL REVIEW *and* THE ELEMENTARY SCHOOL JOURNAL

No. 19   May 1922

THE SELECTIVE CHARACTER OF AMERICAN SECONDARY EDUCATION

THE SELECTIVE CHARACTER OF AMERICAN SECONDARY EDUCATION

By

GEORGE SYLVESTER COUNTS

THE UNIVERSITY OF CHICAGO

CHICAGO, ILLINOIS

ACKNOWLEDGMENTS

Many persons have contributed to the success of this study, and, while it is quite impossible to name all those who have helped in one way or another from the securing of the data to the reading of the manuscript, the writer wishes particularly to express his appreciation of the kindly co-operation of the following workers in the field without which the study would not have been possible: Assistant Superintendent G. M. Laselle, Principal James C. Moore, Principal H. J. Hanson, Dr. A. C. Sides, Mr. Frank M. Ham, Mrs. Florence F. Batchelder, Miss Katherine A. Flanagan, and Miss Harriet F. Lambert of Bridgeport; Superintendent W. H. Holmes of Mt. Vernon; Assistant Superintendent W. J. S. Bryan and Principals William M. Butler, Stephen A. Douglas, John J. Maddox, Armand R. Miller, John R. Powell, H. H. Ryan, and Frank L. Williams of St. Louis; Vocational Director S. E. Fleming and Principals Karl F. Adams, L. P. Bennett, F. L. Cassidy, V. K. Froula, O. L. Luther, and James A. Reed of Seattle; and Morton Snyder formerly Principal of the University of Chicago High School and Principal Lewis Perry of the Phillips-Exeter Academy.

TABLE OF CONTENTS

LIST OF TABLES

ix

LIST OF FIGURES

PART I. INTRODUCTION

CHAPTER I

THE PROBLEM

For two generations the public high school in the United States has grown at such a rapid rate as to give it a unique place in the history of educational institutions. Appearing late in the first quarter of the nineteenth century, it at once entered into a struggle for survival with the dominant secondary school of the time, the private academy. For a half-century the high school maintained itself with more or less success, and was well established by 1870. During the fifty years that have elapsed in the meantime it has expanded in a manner quite without precedent. From 1890 to 1918 the number of high schools reporting to the Bureau at Washington increased from 2,526 to 13,951; the number of pupils in attendance from 202,963 to 1,645,171; and the number of teachers from 9,120 to 81,034. At the same time the population of the United States increased from 62,622,250 to approximately 105,253,000. Thus while the high-school enrolment increased 711 per cent the total population increased but 68 per cent. From year to year this institution has constantly attracted a larger and larger proportion of the children of high-school age in the nation.

This remarkable expansion of the high school is impressively pictured in Figure I in which the high-school enrolment is compared with that of the elementary school and with the total population at five-year periods from 1870 to 1918. The curve for the high school begins with 1871 instead of the year before, because data for 1870 are not available. That the curves for the three series may be easily compared they are based on index numbers, derived as indicated in the explanation of the diagram. It is seen at once that the high-school curve is distinctly different from the curves for the elementary school and the total population. The latter are almost identical and show a steady progression of the arithmetical type. The increase of the elementary-school enrolment for fifty years has evidently been a function of the general population increase. The curve for the high school, on the other hand, is of the geometrical order. For the first decade, from 1870 to 1880, the increase in high-school enrolment actually failed to keep pace with the growth of population; during the following decade the two series were parallel; and since 1890 the high-school enrolment has been growing at a rate constantly accelerated from period to period without showing any marked dependence on the general increase of population. Truly the American public high school occupies a unique place among educational institutions.

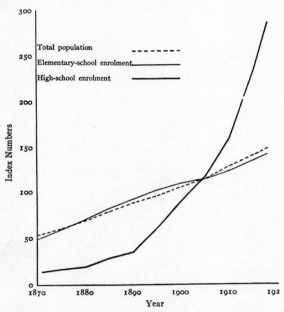

FIG. 1.—Showing relative rates of increase in the total population, the number of pupils enrolled in the elementary school, and the number of students enrolled in the public high school, United States, 1870–1918. The index numbers are found by dividing the total population and the total enrolment for each date by the respective averages for the eleven periods considered. (Adapted from *U.S. Bureau of Education Bulletin, No. 19*, 1920, p. 47.)

And the end is not yet, as the merest glance at the high-school curve shows. In view of the direction it is taking today, apparently there is but one ultimate limitation to the increase in the high-school registration, and that is to be found in the number of children of high-school age in the population. We are already hearing murmurings about universal secondary education. It is pointed out that, in spite of the very rapid increase in high-school enrolment in recent years, there are enrolled today in our secondary schools, both public and private, only about

2,000,000 out of a total of approximately 8,300,000 children of high-school age in the nation. Some of our states are passing compulsory education laws that break with our tradition of compulsory education for the elementary period only, and point toward some measure of compulsory secondary education.

The conception of secondary education as education for the selected few, whether by birth or by talent, appears to be giving ground before the assaults of political democracy and the demands of a society of increasing complexity and wealth. Some are saying that, as public elementary education is no longer education for the masses, but rather education for childhood, so secondary education is no longer education for the classes, but rather education for adolescence. Thus in a statement made by the teachers of the Washington Irving High School for Girls in New York City in 1911 we find these words: "A public high school differs from an elementary school chiefly in the age of its children." Such a statement marks a new era in the history of secondary education.

In view of the remarkable increase in high-school enrolment and the changing conception of secondary education, it is becoming increasingly pertinent to inquire into the character of that student population which is attracted to the public high school. And it is the object of the present study to make such an inquiry, at least in so far as the city high school is concerned.

Is it true in practice that the public high school differs from the elementary school chiefly in the age of its children? Has the revolutionary increase in the high-school enrolment involved the abandonment of the selective principle in secondary education? And more specifically, from what occupational groups do the high-school students come? Are all social classes fairly well represented? Is the public high school popular in the real sense of the word, or are we maintaining at public expense a secondary institution for certain favored classes in spite of this extraordinary growth of recent decades? Are the children of immigrants, the very children whose years in high school might be expected to yield the largest returns to both the individual and society, to be found in the high school in proportionate numbers? Do the various immigrant groups exhibit special or characteristic traits toward high-school attendance? What is the reaction of the negro toward the public high school? How are the children from the different social, cultural, and racial elements grouping themselves in the high school with respect to the courses pursued? What are their expectations following graduation? From the standpoint of securing a secondary education is it fortunate or unfortunate to be the last-born? How great is the misfortune of losing one or both parents? What is the psychological equipment of those children who enter high school, as compared with those who do not? Who remain for graduation? In a word, what is the sociological and psychological character of the public high school population? Many of these questions have received consideration in other investigations—they all receive some attention in the present study, although the emphasis throughout is sociological rather than psychological.

It is clear that a thorough study of the high-school population is fundamental to the solution of all problems of organization and administration. The high-school student should furnish the point of departure for the wise determination of high-school policy and practice.

It is equally clear that an adequate social interpretation of the high school must rest upon relatively complete knowledge of the social sources from which its population comes, as well as on comparatively general agreement as to the objectives at which the school is aiming. The contact which the high school makes with the social order through the Freshman year is as significant as that which it makes through the graduating class. With the former are bound up questions of large social import, such as the relation of groups to groups, the stability of classes, the source of leadership, and the distribution of power, at least in so far as these matters may be affected by the secondary school. It is hoped that this study will make some contribution toward such an interpretation.

CHAPTER II

SOURCE AND COLLECTION OF THE DATA

In attacking this problem it was decided to take a complete census of the high-school population in several American cities representing different parts of the country. Obviously, returns from a single high school drawing its students from a single quarter of one of our large cities would not be satisfactory because of the well-known tendency of populations of similar social and economic standing to gravitate to the same section of the city. It was thought desirable to study a community sufficiently complex to present all the more important groups (except the agricultural) found in modern society, and sufficiently large to provide representation of each of the groups adequate for statistical purposes. For these reasons an entire city was studied in each case.

THE GROUPS STUDIED

The cities chosen for the central part of the study were Seattle, Washington; St. Louis, Missouri; Bridgeport, Connecticut; and Mt. Vernon, New York. These four cities were selected primarily because it was found possible to secure data from them, and not because they represent an ideal combination to picture the condition of secondary education in the United States. The writer has worked in St. Louis, Seattle, and Bridgeport in one capacity or another that has brought him in touch with the public schools in these places. It was, therefore, possible to get that degree of co-operation in gathering the data that is necessary to insure reasonable accuracy in so comprehensive a study. Mt. Vernon was chosen because records from the National Intelligence Tests were already available for all students in the elementary school and the first year of the high school. Nevertheless, a fairly good case can be made out for the selection of these cities from the standpoint of their representative character, as will be pointed out in the following chapter.

In addition to the census of the high-school population, data were secured from certain other groups in Seattle, Bridgeport, and Mt. Vernon, which it was thought would throw light on our problem. In Seattle a study was made of children of high-school age at work in the commercial and industrial plants of that city. In Bridgeport facts were secured from three additional groups of children: (1) those attending

5

the evening high school; (2) those enrolled in the state trade school, an institution offering an intensive and practical two-year course in some fifteen trades and operating under the provisions of the Smith-Hughes Act; and (3) those found in the compulsory continuation classes of the evening school, an interesting Connecticut institution enrolling children between the ages of fourteen and sixteen years who have left the regular day-school to go to work without having completed the elementary grades. In Mt. Vernon the sixth grade was included in making the study. Facts from these non-high-school groups are of exceptional value in interpreting the data from the high-school students.

Also for the purpose of getting some idea of the character of that large body of young folk attending the private secondary schools of the country, data were secured from the University of Chicago High School and the Phillips-Exeter Academy. A separate chapter will be set aside for the analysis and interpretation of data secured from these sources.

THE METHOD OF PROCEDURE

With a few exceptions a uniform procedure was followed in getting the data. In the schools, both high and otherwise, a card similar to the one reproduced below was filled out by all the children in attendance on a certain day.

MOUNT VERNON HIGH SCHOOL

Date...

Name.. Sex............. Age ....yrs......mos.

Grade in high school..................................... Course............................

Is there a telephone in your home or the home in which you live? ....

Language or languages spoken in your home ....

Information about father: Living?........ Country of birth....................................

    Present occupation............................. Where or for whom does he work?.........

    .... Is he either owner or part owner of the business in which he works?...............

    Occupation while alive or while working if not living or working now?........................

Information about mother: Living?......... Country of birth.............................

    Helping to support family?............ If so, how?..

If you have a guardian, give his occupation...

How many brothers and sisters have you?............... How many are older than you?.........

Do you expect to complete your high school course?...

If not, why not?.. What do you intend to do

after graduation from high school?...

To each teacher in charge of a "home room" was sent the number of cards required. Along with this set of cards went a single card filled out for a hypothetical case, and the following set of instructions:

The chief object of this investigation is to discover the extent to which the students in the public high school are drawn from the different population groups. The items relating to the parents are, therefore, to be regarded as the most significant. The others are of subordinate interest.

The high-school student should fill in every blank (provided, of course, the question is pertinent to his case) except the one for his name. It is not necessary to have the student's name, if care is taken to fill out the card accurately and fully. This item would be of value only in case it should be found desirable to refer the card to the student for more complete and definite information.

In answering the questions relating to the occupation of the father, it is particularly important that the answer be as definite as possible, in order that the father may at least be accurately placed in one of the larger occupational divisions, such as, unskilled labor, semi-skilled labor, skilled labor, the clerical occupations, personal service, the professions, the managerial and employing occupations. There are two types of answers to be avoided. There is the vague and indefinite answer such as "shipyards." Unless this is accompanied by a statement of what the father does in the shipyards, the answer is without value. In the second place, the student may use a term which has several meanings, such as "agent" or "engineer." Obviously such an answer may be variously construed. There are many different kinds of agents and several different kinds of engineers. The questions concerning the father's place of work and his ownership in the business are for the purpose of checking and clarifying the response to the question about occupation. It may be helpful in securing accurate information to consult the following list which, according to the United States Census for 1910, includes the principal occupations of the people of the United States:

Actors	Cabinet-makers	Dairy farmers
Agents, general	Candy-makers	Deliverymen
Agents, insurance	Canvassers	Dentists
Agents, railway station	Carpenters	Designers
Agents, real estate	Carriage drivers	Detectives, Marshals, etc.
Architects	Chambermaids	Domestics, general
Authors	Chauffeurs	Draftsmen
Baggagemen	Chemists	Dressmakers
Bakers	Cigarmakers	Druggists
Barbers, Hairdressers	Clay- and stone-workers	Dyers
Bartenders	Clergymen	Editors
Blacksmiths	Clerks, store	Electricians
Boarding-house keepers	Clerks, other	Electrotypers, Stereotypers
Boiler-makers	Collectors	Elevator tenders
Bookkeepers	Cooks	Engineers, civil
Brakemen	Commercial travelers	Locomotive
Brokers, commercial	Compositors	Mining
Brokers, stock	Conductors, steam railway	Stationary
Builders	Conductors, street railway	Engravers
Butchers	Coopers	Express messengers

Farmers
Filers, Grinders
Firemen, fire department
　Locomotive
　Stationary
Fishermen
Foremen, manufacturing
Foresters
Furnacemen
Gardeners, Florists
Glassblowers
Hatmakers
Hostlers
Hotelkeepers
Housekeepers, Stewards
Janitors
Jewelers
Laborers, domestic
　Farm
　Garden
　General
　Public Service
　Railroad
　Store
Launderers (not in laundry)
Lawyers, Judges
Lithographers
Longshoremen
Lumbermen

Machinists
Mail carriers
Mail clerks, railway
　Other
Managers, manufacturing
Manufacturers
Masons, brick and stone
Merchants, retail
　Wholesale
Millers, grain, etc.
Milliners
Miners
Molders, Founders
Motormen
Musicians
Nurses, not trained
　Others, trained
Officials, city
　State and U.S.
Opticians
Paperhangers
Pattern-makers
Photographers
Physicians, Surgeons
Plasterers
Plumbers
Policemen
Porters (not store)
Postmasters

Pressmen, printing
Professors, college
Reporters
Restaurant-keepers
Roofers
Sailors (U.S. Service)
　Others
Salesmen, and saleswomen
Saloon-keepers
Sawyers
Sewers (factory)
Shoemakers (not factory)
Showmen
Soldiers
Stenographers
Stonecutters
Surgeons, veterinary
Switchmen, Yardmen
Tailors
Teachers
Teamsters
Telegraph operators
Telephone operators
Tinsmiths
Undertakers
Upholsterers
Watchmakers
Waiters

Of course it should be made clear to the students that this information is strictly confidential and will not be used in any personal connection whatsoever. It would be well at the outset to state to them the purpose of the investigation and the necessity of having accurate information. Their co-operation is necessary in securing it.

In order to clarify any misunderstanding concerning the meanings of the questions, the card for a hypothetical case is filled out and accompanies this explanation.

Be sure to allow the students sufficient time to answer every question with care, even though it may be necessary in some cases to permit them to take the card home to consult the parents.

Each card should be examined after the student has filled it out in order to correct any obvious errors and to see that all questions are answered. Your help in this way will be greatly appreciated.

There were, however, some exceptions to the plan of procedure just outlined. The cards used in Seattle and St. Louis did not include the questions concerning the language spoken in the home and the country of the parent's birth. But they did include questions relating to student self-support which were discarded in the latter part of the investigation. Also the inquiry about the telephone in the home was made only in Bridgeport and Mt. Vernon. In Seattle and St. Louis the father's occupation three years ago was requested for the purpose of determining the extent of occupational change during high-school attendance. In one of the Seattle high schools (the first in which the study was attempted) an effort was made to get definite information as to the father's income, but without success. The question was entirely too personal and was consequently dropped from the card lest it imperil the accuracy of the returns to the other questions. Also in the first Seattle high school the questions about brothers and sisters did not appear on the card, with the result that the returns on this item are not complete for the city of Seattle. In Bridgeport and Mt. Vernon children did fill in the blank for the name, and there seemed to be no objection to it. In St. Louis and in four of the six Seattle schools this was not required of the students. In Mt. Vernon the set of instructions did not accompany the cards to the teachers. In view of the size of the school and the consequent greater intimacy of contact between the supervisory staff and the teacher, it was thought sufficient to send to each teacher merely the card filled out for a hypothetical case. In concluding this enumeration of the exceptions to the general method of procedure, it should be pointed out that the cards used in the evening high school, the trade school, and the compulsory continuation classes in Bridgeport and the Mt. Vernon sixth grade were modified in each instance to meet the requirements of the situation.

The facts for the children of high-school age at work in Seattle were obtained through personal interviews by investigators who went into all the commercial and industrial establishments of the city in which it was known that such children were at work. This was done through the co-operation of the Seattle Chamber of Commerce. For the most part the investigators were teachers in the public schools of the city.

In Bridgeport and Mt. Vernon the sociological data were supplemented by intelligence test records. In the former city the Chapman-Welles Junior- and Senior-High School Classification Test was given to the four groups of children already mentioned. To the compulsory continuation classes and the children in the trade school, the test was given by the writer, while the giving of the tests in the day and evening high schools was under the direction of high-school supervisors and

teachers who were more or less experienced in giving tests. In Mt.
Vernon the National Intelligence Tests, Scale B, Form I, were given by
persons within the system.

The data for the study were collected during the years 1919, 1920,
and 1921. The cards were filled out in the Seattle high schools at
intervals during the months of November and December of 1919, and
January of 1920. The children of high-school age at work in that city
were interviewed during the Christmas vacation of the school year
1919–20. The data from St. Louis were secured in December, 1920.
In Bridgeport the cards for both the day and evening high schools and
the continuation classes were filled out in December, 1920, and those for
the trade school in February, 1921. The intelligence tests were given
there in December, 1920, and in January, February, and March, 1921.
In Mt. Vernon the tests were administered in October, 1920, and the
cards were filled out the following May (1921).

NUMBER OF CASES STUDIED

In getting the returns from the high schools an effort was made to
obtain responses from all children in attendance on that day. The
number filling out the cards in each city is indicated in Table I. Thus
for this basic part of the study there are 17,992 cases. Of the 8,264
cases reported for the St. Louis high schools, 727, constituting the entire
enrolment of one of the schools, are negroes. This very interesting
group will receive special attention in a separate chapter.

TABLE I

NUMBER AND SEX OF HIGH-SCHOOL STUDENTS FILLING OUT THE INFORMATION CARD
IN EACH OF THE CITIES

CITY	NUMBER OF HIGH-SCHOOL STUDENTS		
	Girls	Boys	Total
Bridgeport................................	1,220	1,037	2,257
Mt. Vernon...............................	516	568	1,084
St. Louis..................................	4,462	3,802	8,264
Seattle....................................	3,572	2,815	6,387
Total................................	9,770	8,222	17,992

The number of children in the special groups outside the regular
day high school from whom information of a similar character was
received is shown in Table II. No one of these groups is very large.
Neither is any claim of complete returns made except for the trade

school and the Mt. Vernon sixth grade.   In the other three cases the most that can be claimed is that random samplings have been secured. The number of children of high-school age at work in Seattle was certainly

TABLE II

NUMBER AND SEX OF CHILDREN FILLING OUT THE INFORMATION CARD IN EACH OF THE NON-HIGH-SCHOOL GROUPS

GROUP	NUMBER OF CHILDREN		
	Girls	Boys	Total
Children of high-school age at work in Seattle..........................	249	265	514
Bridgeport Evening High School........	147	96	243
State Trade School at Bridgeport........	14	184	198
Bridgeport Compulsory Continuation Classes..............................	305	274	579
Mt. Vernon Sixth Grade...............	341	398	739
Total...........................	1,056	1,217	2,273

much greater than 514.   In the Bridgeport Evening High School there were approximately one thousand students.   Many of them were far beyond the high-school age.   But only students twenty-one years of age or less were included in this study.   Likewise returns were secured from only about 50 per cent of the children in the compulsory continuation classes.   In each instance, however, those studied are thought to be quite representative of the group.

TABLE III

NUMBER AND DISTRIBUTION OF CHILDREN TAKING THE INTELLIGENCE TESTS

GROUP	NUMBER OF CHILDREN		
	Girls	Boys	Total
Bridgeport High School................	1,362	1,169	2,531
Bridgeport Evening High School.........	86	95	181
State Trade School at Bridgeport........	9	164	173
Bridgeport Compulsory Continuation Classes..............................	220	201	421
Mt. Vernon High School...............	192	216	408
Total...........................	1,869	1,845	3,714

The groups to which the intelligence tests were administered were not completely identical with those for which the sociological data were secured, because some days or weeks or even months elapsed in each case between filling out the cards and taking the test, or vice versa. The number taking the test in each group is shown in Table III. It will be noted that in some cases the number taking the test is larger than the number filling out the cards, and in other cases the reverse is true. However, this is a matter of no importance when group results alone are wanted.

ACCURACY

The accuracy of the data is of course a matter of fundamental importance. Are the returns accurate or at least of such a character as to guarantee reliable conclusions? Let us first consider the sociological data.

The first question here pertains to the character of the information requested and the wording on the card. Is the high-school student in possession of the information asked for? He undoubtedly is, with the possible exception of the information relating to the father's ownership of the business in which he works. And even here, the responses to the other questions about the father's occupation make it possible in most cases to arrive at a reasonably satisfactory single result. Are the questions definite and do they call for specific information? Here again the answer is in the affirmative. Is there good reason for suspecting that the high-school student might color his replies to some of the questions? Probably in some cases there would be a temptation to put a more favorable construction on the father's occupation than the facts would warrant. This temptation, however, was largely removed in St. Louis and in the four Seattle high schools where the student's name was not called for. Thus the returns from Bridgeport and Mt. Vernon may be checked against those from the other two cities. It is also highly probable that the average high-school student is over-optimistic about his prospects. Consequently little weight should be attached to his stated intentions following graduation from high school, as an index of what he really is going to do. But, even so, as a statement of his intention, as an idea that occurred to him for a reason, it does in the writer's opinion have some validity. And no other claim for accuracy will be made regarding it during the course of the study. Did the students make a serious effort to fill out the cards and furnish the desired information? They evidently did in the great majority of cases. It is true that in almost every high school one or two boys took the whole matter as a great joke and taxed their ingenuity to the limit to give the least possible bit of valuable information and the largest possible amount of nonsense. But, on the whole, the replies showed careful attention to the work in hand and a serious effort to co-operate in providing the information.

A second general question pertains to the collection of the data. Is there any good reason for believing that the returns are from a selected group? On the whole the answer is a negative one. In each high school, with the exception of the Soldan High School of St. Louis, the day on which the census was taken was a normal day and the cards were received from practically all the students in attendance. At the Soldan the cards were filled out the day before the Christmas vacation and there were many absent, particularly among the Seniors. Subsequently an effort was made to complete the census, but evidently there was a considerable number of students in this high school from whom no cards were received. And it happens that incompleteness at this point has probably colored the returns from St. Louis to a small degree, because the Soldan High School serves a rather homogeneous and select middle-class constituency. It should therefore be remembered, when we note the social composition of the high-school population of St. Louis, that our figures do not give the non-labor groups as large a representation as they probably have. In collecting data from the non-high-school children there is no good reason for suspecting bias. For obvious reasons, in the case of the evening high school in Bridgeport, the study was limited to students of twenty-one years of age and under. Except in those cases where it is expressly stated to the contrary, the returns apparently are complete and unselected.

CHAPTER III

CHARACTER OF THE CITIES CHOSEN FOR THE STUDY

Before going into an analysis of the results of the investigation, it will be well to examine briefly into the character of the cities from which the data were secured. This is a matter of prime importance in a study such as this one, in which the sociological interest is prominent.

It has already been intimated that the study was not undertaken in these cities primarily because of their representative character. They were studied because they presented the opportunity. They were studied because it was possible to study them. Nevertheless an examination of the facts will show them to be fairly representative of the country.

GEOGRAPHICAL AND HISTORICAL

In Seattle we have a city of the Pacific Coast, representative of the North and the far West. St. Louis lies between the North and the South, and between the East and the West, exhibiting in some measure the characteristics of all. Bridgeport, an Atlantic seaport and industrial center, and Mt. Vernon, a growing community just outside the city of New York, stand for the East. To be sure, the real South is not adequately represented; neither is the Great Lakes region; nor the plains states. Furthermore, Boston and New England might not be satisfied with Bridgeport. But it must be admitted that these four cities do represent different parts of our country.

No one of our cities can trace its history back to 1607 or 1620, although the city of Bridgeport does claim that there was a settlement of white people made in territory constituting the site of modern Bridgeport as early as 1639. It was not, however, until 1836 that the city was incorporated. St. Louis is one of the oldest cities west of the Alleghanies, reaching back to the days of Marquette and Joliet and La Salle. It was incorporated as a city in 1822, and thus holds the distinction of having been the first city incorporated west of the Mississippi. Naturally the rise of Seattle came later as a part of the development of the Oregon country. Yet its date of incorporation goes back to 1869. Mt. Vernon, though possessing a considerable history as a town, did not become a city until 1892.

An examination of Table IV is of interest at this point.   It shows the
increase of population in each of the four cities from 1870 to 1920.
The facts here presented reveal important and significant differences
among the cities.   Clearly they are not all of the same type.   Fifty
years ago St. Louis was a great urban center of more than 300,000
inhabitants.   Seattle, on the other hand, a city that likes to call itself

TABLE IV

INCREASE OF POPULATION IN EACH OF THE FOUR CITIES FROM 1870 TO 1920

Year	Bridgeport	Mt. Vernon	St. Louis	Seattle
1870.....................	18,969	2,700	310,864	1,107
1880.....................	27,643	4,586	350,518	3,533
1890.....................	48,866	10,830	451,770	42,837
1900.....................	70,996	21,228	575,238	80,671
1910.....................	102,054	30,919	687,029	237,194
1920.....................	143,555	42,726	772,897	315,312

the New York of the Pacific today, was at that time nothing but an
assemblage of shacks about a trading post, housing scarcely more than
a thousand souls.   St. Louis has been growing gradually during this
period, but not so rapidly as most American cities, while the growth of
Seattle, especially during the decade from 1900 to 1910, has been nothing
short of phenomenal.   In Bridgeport and Mt. Vernon we have two
cities exhibiting the steady and rapid growth characteristic of industrial
centers developing in the well-populated sections of our country during
the last half-century.   They are intermediate between Seattle and
St. Louis.

For the purposes of this study it is fortunate that we have cities
showing these different rates of growth.   In Seattle we find a vigorous,
adventurous, and youthful population, composed of elements lured to
this metropolis of the Northwest from the states to the east, and among
whom the native son is rare indeed.   Here society is less stable; the
lines between social classes are not rigidly drawn.   Everybody works.
Seattle is not a city of magnificent residences.   In St. Louis, on the other
hand, we have an altogether different situation.   The city is old, in
American and middle western terms, and the population has not increased
rapidly during the last generation.   Society is more stable.   The lines
between classes are more closely drawn, although the people are less
aware of those lines in St. Louis than in Seattle.   Habit and custom
have assumed their expected rôle.   The old families do exist and St. Louis

does have its magnificent residences. It is a place in which to live as
well as to work. These differences are of the largest significance for the
study.

THE PEOPLE

A study of the people inhabiting these four cities shows us a population almost as varied and complex as that of the nation itself. In Table
V are the facts pertaining to race and nationality as given in the latest

TABLE V

RACIAL AND ETHNIC COMPOSITION OF THE POPULATIONS OF THE FOUR CITIES
ACCORDING TO THE CENSUS OF 1910

RACE OR NATIONALITY	BRIDGEPORT		MT. VERNON		ST. LOUIS		SEATTLE	
	Number	Per-centage	Number	Per-centage	Number	Per-centage	Number	Per-centage
Native white (native parentage)............	27,156	26.6	11,433	37.0	269,836	39.2	105,784	44.6
Native white (foreign and mixed parentage)......	37,314	36.6	10,539	34.0	246,946	35.9	61,134	25.8
Foreign-born white.......	36,180	35.5	8,029	26.0	125,706	18.4	60,835	25.6
Negro.................	1,332	1.2	896	2.9	43,960	6.4	2,296	1.0
Indians, Chinese, Japanese, etc..................	72	.1	22	.1	581	.1	7,145	3.0
Total..............	102,054	100.0	30,919	100.0	687,029	100.0	237,194	100.0

available census, that of 1910. A glance at this table is illuminating.
Bridgeport is one of the most foreign of American cities with only 26.6
per cent of its inhabitants reported as native white of native parentage.
Practically the entire remainder is either foreign born or of foreign and
mixed parentage, since the colored races have but a negligible representation. At the other extreme is Seattle which is one of the least foreign
of our cities with 44.6 per cent of its inhabitants of native white parentage.
In St. Louis is found a different situation. The native white stock is
well represented, as is also the native white of foreign and mixed parentage; whereas the proportion of foreign-born white is the lowest for the
four cities, and is decidedly low for the larger American cities. Mt.
Vernon presents no distinctive features. Finally it should be noted
that St. Louis has a good representation of negroes, while the Orientals,
particularly the Chinese and the Japanese, constitute an important
element in the population of Seattle.

But how are the different immigrant strains represented? Do we
find both the "old" and the "new" immigration? In Table VI is the
answer. Here the immigrants and native whites of foreign parentage
are grouped according to the country from which they or both their

parents have come. Again each of the cities presents individual features. In Bridgeport the most numerous immigrant group comes from that polyglot section of Europe formerly known as the Austro-Hungarian Empire; in Mt. Vernon the Italians hold first place; in St. Louis almost one-half of the immigrants are of German stock; while in Seattle the immigrants from the Scandinavian countries constitute the largest single group, as classified. In so far as the immigrant population is

TABLE VI

NATIVITY OF FOREIGN-BORN WHITES AND PARENTS OF NATIVE WHITES OF FOREIGN PARENTAGE IN THE FOUR CITIES (1910)

COUNTRY	BRIDGEPORT		MT. VERNON		ST. LOUIS		SEATTLE	
	Number	Per-centage	Number	Per-centage	Number	Per-centage	Number	Per-centage
Austria-Hungary.........	16,883	25.8	426	2.8	28,377	9.8	2,901	2.9
Canada.................	2,002	3.1	345	2.2	3,138	1.1	14,317	14.3
Great Britain...........	6,383	9.8	1,367	8.9	11,270	3.9	13,025	13.0
Germany...............	6,136	9.4	3,924	25.5	138,094	47.9	13,898	13.9
Ireland.................	13,070	20.0	2,403	15.6	41,326	14.3	7,294	7.3
Italy..................	7,420	11.3	4,371	28.3	11,360	3.9	4,399	4.4
Russia.................	6,242	9.6	933	6.0	23,868	8.3	3,513	3.5
Scandinavia............	3,725	5.7	537	3.5	2,926	1.0	28,353	28.5
All others..............	3,437	5.3	1,112	7.2	28,350	9.8	12,209	12.2
Total..............	65,298	100.0	15,418	100.0	288,709	100.0	99,909	100.0

concerned, Seattle represents the "old" immigration, the immigration from the north and west of Europe, with only 10.8 per cent from Austria-Hungary, Italy, and Russia. In St. Louis, which is also predominantly a center for the "old" immigration, 22 per cent of its immigrants are from these three countries of the south and east of Europe. In Mt. Vernon this percentage rises to 37.1; and in Bridgeport to 46.7. Thus it is clear that from the standpoint of race and nationality these four cities give a fairly complete picture of urban America.

OCCUPATIONS

For the purposes of this study perhaps the most important information about the population pertains to the occupations. In what occupations are the people of these four cities engaged? The facts on this point, according to the census of 1910, are found in Table VII. An examination of this table shows the variety of occupational interest characteristic of American cities. Of the nine great occupational divisions recognized by the census the seven which might be expected in urban communities are proportionately represented in these four cities. To be sure, the percentage of persons engaged in public service, according to the census classification, is quite small in each case, but this is characteristic of cities generally. Although American cities are as a rule predominantly industrial, and although the cities here studied are no exceptions to this rule, yet the table shows marked differences among them in the proportion of the inhabitants engaged in the manufacturing and mechanical occupations. At the one extreme is Bridgeport with over 60 per cent of its people so engaged, and at the other is Seattle with scarcely more than 30 per cent. St. Louis occupies a middle ground.

TABLE VII

TOTAL NUMBER OF PERSONS TEN YEARS OF AGE OR OVER ENGAGED IN EACH
SPECIFIED OCCUPATION IN EACH OF THE FOUR CITIES (1910)

OCCUPATIONAL DIVISION	BRIDGEPORT		MT. VERNON		ST. LOUIS		SEATTLE	
	Number	Per- centage	Number	Per- centage	Number	Per- centage	Number	Per- centage
Agriculture, forestry, and animal husbandry......	477	1.0	120	1.0	2,203	.7	4,460	3.6
Extracting of minerals....	26	.1	20	.2	1,621	.5	1,915	1.6
Manufacturing and me- chanical industry......	30,696	61.4	4,147	33.6	133,151	41.5	39,639	32.4
Transportation..........	2,788	5.6	939	7.6	28,079	8.7	17,116	14.0
Trade...................	5,053	10.1	2,330	18.9	54,117	16.9	20,266	16.6
Public service	681	1.4	169	1.3	5,858	1.8	2,585	2.1
Professional service	2,259	4.5	1,173	9.5	15,952	5.0	8,762	7.2
Domestic and personal service	4,531	9.1	2,107	17.0	46,288	14.5	17,289	14.1
Clerical occupations	3,407	6.8	1,347	10.9	33,445	10.4	10,253	8.4
Total..............	49,918	100.0	12,352	100.0	320,714	100.0	122,285	100.0

The range here presented is almost as great as that to be found among the larger American cities. Bridgeport is an industrial center of the clearest type, while Seattle is a community with a greater variety of interests, in which industrial development is in its earlier stages. In the latter city there are almost as many persons engaged in trade and transportation as in industry. This is to be expected in a great seaport in which the commercial interest is naturally very large. The table shows important differences in the proportion of the populations engaged in the other occupations, but enough has been said to make it clear that these four cities are fairly representative of American cities with respect to occupational interests.

A slight additional comment of a more specific nature concerning the character of the industrial undertakings in each of the four cities will be of value, because of the dominant rôle played by industry in the American city. To an appreciable degree industry gives the city its tone.

Almost every conceivable thing is manufactured in Bridgeport from collar buttons to field artillery. Its most important products are corsets; foundry and machine-shop products; electrical machinery and supplies of all sorts; cutlery and tools; and copper, tin, and sheet-iron products. In addition, the people of Bridgeport make automobiles, carriages, cigars, bicycles, boots and shoes, carpets, firearms, paint, patent medicines, hosiery, sewing machines, silverware, typewriters, and a host of other things. Mt. Vernon is largely a place of residence for persons working in New York City. Yet there are several concerns engaged in the manufacture of motor vehicles, optical instruments, silver products, shirt waists, etc. St. Louis manufactures a great variety of goods. The products in whose manufacture the largest numbers of workers are engaged are boots and shoes; printing and publishing; men's and women's clothing; foundry and machine-shop products; furniture; lumber and timber products; carriages and wagons; pottery and terra cotta; stoves and furnaces; copper, tin, and sheet-iron products; and in a happier day great quantities of liquors and stimulating beverages. Seattle, though less given to manufacture, does produce many things. Quite naturally first among them are lumber and timber products. Others are foundry and machine-shop products; confectionery; copper, tin, and sheet-iron products; flour and grist-mill products; and furniture. There are also a goodly number of persons engaged in printing and publishing; the slaughtering and meat-packing industries are developing; and during the war Seattle developed into a great shipbuilding center.

VALUE OF PROPERTY

No picture of a city is complete without some reference to the value of its property. This is especially true in any study of public education, an enterprise dependent on taxation for support.

According to a special report of the census in 1919 the estimated true value of property per capita in St. Louis was $1,497.85, while the average for the group of American cities having over 500,000 inhabitants, the group to which St. Louis belongs, was $1,584.51. The corresponding figures for Seattle were $1,630.88 and $1,617.88; for Bridgeport, $1,592.05 and $1,353.25; and for Mt. Vernon, $1,286.28 and $1,234.30. According to these estimates, no one of the four cities represents either of the extremes of wealth or of poverty. With the exception of St. Louis, they are slightly above the average for cities of their class, but the superiority is not marked in any case. All appear to be cities of moderate wealth.

THE HIGH SCHOOL AND CHILDREN OF HIGH-SCHOOL AGE

A final question and one most significant for this study pertains to the high school itself in these four cities. What proportion of the children of high-school age (taken somewhat arbitrarily in this study to include all children from fourteen to seventeen years of age) are enrolled in the high school? The facts bearing on this point appear in Table VIII in which is given the estimated number of children of high-school

TABLE VIII

NUMBER OF CHILDREN OF HIGH-SCHOOL AGE, NUMBER OF CHILDREN IN THE PUBLIC HIGH SCHOOLS, AND PERCENTAGE OF CHILDREN OF HIGH-SCHOOL AGE IN THE PUBLIC HIGH SCHOOLS IN EACH OF THE FOUR CITIES AND IN THE UNITED STATES IN 1918

	Bridgeport	Mt. Vernon	St. Louis	Seattle	United States
Children of high-school age.	10,618	3,169	59,324	23,368	8,053,872
Children in public high schools................	1,990	1,010	10,586	6,719	1,645,171
Percentage of children in public high schools......	18.7	31.9	17.8	28.8	20.4

age in each of the cities and in the nation in 1918, the number of children enrolled in the public high schools according to the report of the Bureau of Education for the school year 1917–18, and the percentage that the latter is of the former. No claim is made of absolute accuracy for these figures, but they are unquestionably approximately correct.

The table shows that two of the cities (Bridgeport and St. Louis) have a somewhat smaller proportion of their children of high-school age in the public high school than the country as a whole; whereas, the other two (Mt. Vernon and Seattle) are markedly above the average practice for the nation. Seattle's record is particularly noteworthy in a city of more than 300,000 inhabitants. In fact there are few cities as large as Seattle having so large a proportion of their children of high-school age in high school. This diversity of practice in a matter which lies at the heart of this study is of large value and reference to this table will be made in later chapters in connection with the analysis and interpretation of the results of the investigation.

PART II. ANALYSIS OF THE DATA

CHAPTER IV

PARENTAL OCCUPATION—CLASSIFICATION

Occupation is the central fact in the lives of the great masses of people. It is the interest that occupies the time and energy of the ordinary person for the major part of his waking hours. In large measure it determines his place of residence, his associates during the working-day, and his more intimate acquaintances and friends of the leisure moments. If pursued for years, it will set its mark on his physical nature and will stamp his mind with its special pattern. It will determine to a considerable degree what he does, what he thinks, and his outlook on life. Increasingly, it seems, a man's occupation in this complex world determines his political affiliations. Consequently this part of the study, setting forth the relation of parental occupation to high-school attendance, may be regarded as its most important contribution.

CLASSIFICATION OF OCCUPATION

The first task encountered as soon as the tabulation of the data commenced was a classification of occupations significant for the purposes of the study. The classification used by the census, recognizing nine great occupational divisions, was inadequate, since it fails to distinguish the various grades of occupations within an industry, due to large-scale production and specialization of function. For example, the division of "manufacturing and mechanical industries" includes in one group those who own the industries, those who manage them, those engaged as technicians, and those who perform the manual labor involving varying degrees of skill. All persons concerned with the production of a particular commodity are grouped together. For the purposes of the census this classification is undoubtedly satisfactory, but for the purposes of this study it is as clearly unsatisfactory.

The ideal classification would be Taussig's famous classification into the five non-competing groups, viz., professional, semi-professional, skilled, semi-skilled, and unskilled occupations. And at the outset of the investigation this classification was chosen, but as the work proceeded it was abandoned. The reasons for this were several. As already indicated this classification is ideal, but it was found exceedingly difficult to use. The lines between the groups are not clearly defined in industry, to say the least. The division between the skilled and the unskilled is certainly no longer altogether clear. However, with relatively complete information for each case, this classification could be attempted with some measure of success; but with the relatively meager information obtained in this study, it was found unworkable without resorting to many arbitrary decisions. It was therefore decided to abandon the attempt at the ideal and adopt a classification that would not give the impression of greater accuracy than the facts would warrant.

The classification finally adopted takes the census classification as a basis, but goes considerably further by breaking up the more complex groups and recognizing certain other groups running directly across the great occupational divisions of the census. The aim is to get classes of reasonable homogeneity from the standpoint of social status, position in the economic order, and intellectual outlook. The result is not altogether satisfactory, and it is far from the ideal, but facts to be presented later show the classification to possess some merit. The groups recognized are as follows:

I. *Proprietors.*—Bankers, brokers, druggists, hotel-owners, landlords, laundry-owners, lumbermen, manufacturers, merchants, mine-owners, publishers, shopkeepers, undertakers, etc.

II. *Professional service.*—Actors, architects, artists, authors, cartoonists, clergymen, dentists, engineers (civil, chemical, electrical, mechanical, mining), journalists, lawyers, librarians, musicians, pharmacists, photographers, physical directors, physicians, social workers, surgeons, teachers, etc.

III. *Managerial service.*—Agents (express, railroad, steamship, telegraph), contractors, foremen, managers, officials and inspectors (private), officials and inspectors (public), superintendents, etc.

IV. *Commercial service.*—Agents (real estate and insurance), buyers, clerks in stores, commercial travelers, salesmen, etc.

V. *Clerical service.*—Accountants, bookkeepers, canvassers, cashiers, clerks (except in stores), collectors, etc.

VI. *Agricultural service.*—Dairymen, farmers, fruit-growers, gardeners, nurserymen, ranchmen, stock-raisers, etc.

VII. *Artisan-proprietors.*—All artisans who own the shops in which they work, including bakers, barbers, blacksmiths, cabinet-makers, cleaners and dyers, cobblers, draftsmen, electricians, machinists, milliners, plumbers, printers, tailors, tinners, etc.

VIII. *Building and related trades.*—Cabinet-makers, carpenters, electricians, glaziers, lathers, masons, plasterers, plumbers, sheet-metal workers, structural iron workers, etc.

IX. *Machine and related trades.*—Anglesmiths, blacksmiths, coppersmiths, designers, draftsmen, engineers (stationary), firemen (except locomotive and fire department), forgemen, founders, machinists, mechanics, millwrights, molders, pattern-makers, tinsmiths, tool-makers, etc.

X. *Printing trades.*—Bookbinders, compositors, electrotypers, engravers, linotypers, pressmen, printers, typesetters, etc.

XI. *Miscellaneous trades in manufacturing and mechanical industries.*—Bakers, bottlers, brewers, cigar-makers, cobblers, coopers, corset-cutters, cutlers, dyers, glass-blowers, grinders, meat-cutters, milliners, platers, shoe-cutters, tailors, tanners, weavers, etc., and machine operatives.

XII. *Transportation service.*—Baggagemen, brakemen, chauffeurs, conductors, draymen, engineers (locomotive and marine), firemen (locomotive and marine), longshoremen, mail carriers, mariners, motormen, sailors, switchmen, yardmen, etc.

XIII. *Public service.*—Detectives, firemen (fire department), guards, marines, marshals, policemen, sailors, soldiers, watchmen, etc.

XIV. *Personal service.*—Barbers, chefs, cooks, doorkeepers, janitors, launderers, porters, sextons, waiters, etc.

XV. *Miners, lumber-workers, and fishermen.*

XVI. *Common labor.*

XVII. *Occupation unknown.*

The first group, the proprietors, includes all the owners of enterprises in whatever field, except the farmers and certain small owners put into Class VII among whom ownership is really secondary to the practice of some skilled trade. This group is the most powerful occupational group in any American community; its members constitute the backbone of the chambers of commerce and similar organizations; it occupies a strategic position in a society based on private property and it controls economic power. In criticism of this classification, it may be said that there is an exceedingly wide range among proprietors. Small shop-keepers are classed with captains of industry and owners of great wealth. There is without question some justice in this criticism, and in the early part of the investigation an effort was made to divide this group into "large" and "small" proprietors. But it was necessary to abandon this effort because of the practical impossibility of introducing this distinction with the available data. Nevertheless ownership does give a certain security even though the business is small. It also gives an outlook on life. While there is superficial heterogeneity, there is fundamental homogeneity throughout the group.

The second group, professional service, requires little comment. It is perhaps in all respects the most homogeneous group in the classification. Its membership is the most "learned" in the community.

In the third group are placed all those persons except owners, who perform any managerial or directing function in all enterprises, whether of a public or private character. In the ordinary industrial organization it includes everything from foreman up to superintendent.

All persons who are active in the buying or selling of goods, except owners, are placed in the fourth group, commercial service. Real estate and insurance agents are all included in this class, even though they are said to be owners or part owners of the business, because in most cases ownership may mean nothing more than the renting of an office. The function performed is that of salesman.

The fifth and sixth divisions require no explanation. Clerical service is rather clearly defined. Agricultural service includes owners, tenants, and laborers. It is, however, a small group in any city and is foreign to the urban economy.

The seventh division, labeled the artisan-proprietors, covers a group of occupations which are really reminiscent of an earlier economic order. Toward the beginning of this study these occupations were not recognized as a separate group, but, as case after case appeared in which the artisan owned his shop, it became clear that some separate provision should be made for them.

The eighth, ninth, tenth, and eleventh divisions include all skilled and semi-skilled workers in the manufacturing and mechanical industries. The first three are among the most homogeneous groups in the entire classification, each being composed of a series of rather closely related and well-known trades. The fourth is a sort of an omnibus class into which all the remaining occupations in this rather broad field, including the machine operatives, are placed. It partakes more of the nature of the semi-skilled trades than any other group in the classification.

The twelfth division includes practically all of the workers·in the field of transportation and is consequently a rather heterogeneous class. The group ranges from longshoremen to railroad engineers and conductors. But since the group is not large in any city it was thought unwise to further complicate the classification through the recognition of another division.

The last five divisions require little comment. The meaning of public service is clear and the same may be said of personal service. The fifteenth division is quite heterogeneous, including the workers in mining, lumbering, and fishing, but it hardly exists in our cities. In the sixteenth division are placed all common laborers from whatever field. It includes all apprentices and helpers, and is as nearly unskilled as any group to be found in modern society. And finally, in the seventeenth and last division, are found all cases in which the father's occupation was not given or in which the data were so meager or indefinite as to make classification impossible.

The data analyzed and interpreted in the following chapters are based on the foregoing classification. In every case where information was given the student was placed in that division to which his father's occupation belongs, even though the father was unemployed at the time, retired for any reason, or not living. In case the father's occupation was not given and the occupation of the guardian was, the classification follows the latter. In no instance was the mother's occupation used for this purpose, even though information concerning both the father and guardian was lacking. This policy is based upon the assumption that the father's occupation is of real significance in determining the social status and outlook of the child almost regardless of whether he is working at the time or not; and that the occupation of the mother is of little importance in this respect. She does what she is able to do, when it is necessary for her to support her children, and the opportunities open to her are limited.

It should be repeated that the occupational classification outlined in this chapter is not ideal in theory, and in practice is less so. In the first place it is extraordinarily difficult to classify occupations today, because the lines between them are not clearly drawn in the economic order and occupations are being formed and reformed in an evolutionary series. The profound changes ushered into industry with the advent of power-driven machinery, marked concentration of labor, and minute specialization have not run their full course. In the second place, in some cases the information given by the student was not so clear as might be desired. These difficulties and shortcomings should not be forgotten while reading the following chapters.

CHAPTER V

PARENTAL OCCUPATION AND TOTAL ENROLMENT

In this chapter will be presented the facts showing the occupations of the fathers or guardians of 17,265 students in the high schools of the four cities. This number does not include the 727 colored children in the Sumner High School in St. Louis, which will receive special treatment in a separate chapter. In interpreting these facts attention will be directed to the number of persons in the general population engaged in the different occupations.

OCCUPATIONAL COMPOSITION OF THE HIGH-SCHOOL POPULATION

The gross data are given in Table IX. All four high-school years are combined. It will be observed that of the 17,265 students, 3,427 have fathers who are occupied as proprietors, 1,629 have fathers engaged in some sort of professional service, and so on.

TABLE IX

OCCUPATIONS OF THE FATHERS OR GUARDIANS OF 17,265 STUDENTS IN THE HIGH SCHOOLS OF FOUR CITIES—ALL FOUR YEARS COMBINED— 1919–20, 1920–21

PARENTAL OCCUPATION	NUMBER					PERCENTAGE				
	Bridge-port	Mt. Vernon	St. Louis	Seattle	Total	Bridge-port	Mt. Vernon	St. Louis	Seattle	Total
Proprietors	451	304	1,603	1,069	3,427	20.0	28.0	21.3	16.7	19.8
Professional service	137	128	661	703	1,629	6.1	11.8	8.8	11.1	9.4
Managerial service	385	181	1,228	1,052	2,846	17.1	16.7	16.3	16.5	16.5
Commercial service	163	122	818	534	1,637	7.2	11.3	10.9	8.3	9.5
Clerical service	98	67	550	281	996	4.3	6.2	7.3	4.4	5.8
Agricultural service	49	11	63	293	416	2.2	1.0	.8	4.6	2.4
Artisan-proprietors	111	56	398	158	723	4.9	5.2	5.3	2.5	4.2
Building trades	116	57	428	724	1,325	5.1	5.3	5.7	11.3	7.7
Machine trades	318	25	432	452	1,227	14.1	2.3	5.7	7.1	7.1
Printing trades	7	4	110	65	186	.3	.4	1.4	1.0	1.1
Miscellaneous trades	139	32	362	121	654	6.2	3.0	4.8	1.9	3.8
Transportation service	77	26	397	346	846	3.4	2.4	5.3	5.4	4.9
Public service	57	9	111	93	270	2.5	.8	1.4	1.5	1.6
Personal service	52	6	81	99	238	2.3	.5	1.1	1.5	1.4
Miners, lumber-workers, fishermen		1	5	60	66		.1	.1	.9	.4
Common labor	38	18	69	88	213	1.7	1.6	.9	1.4	1.2
Unknown	59	37	221	249	566	2.6	3.4	2.9	3.9	3.2
Total	2,257	1,084	7,537	6,387	17,265	100.0	100.0	100.0	100.0	100.0

For comparative purposes the reader should pass to the second part of this table in which the facts are given in percentages. A glance at the percentages for the four cities combined shows four non-labor groups in the lead in the following order: first, the proprietors; second, managerial service; third, commercial service; and fourth, professional service. Among the labor groups only two could be said to be well represented, namely, the building trades and the machine trades. The printing trades, public service, personal service, miners, lumber-workers, fishermen, and common labor have a negligible representation. But 3.2 per cent of the cases are classified as unknown. This means that satisfactory information was received from practically all of the students.

An examination of the remainder of the table, giving the facts for the individual cities, shows considerable variation in the character of the high-school population from city to city. Thus the percentage of proprietors ranges from 16.7 in Seattle to 28.0 in Mt. Vernon; that of professional people from 6.1 in Bridgeport to 11.8 in Mt. Vernon; that of agricultural workers from .8 in St. Louis to 4.6 in Seattle; that of persons engaged in the building trades from 5.1 in Bridgeport to 11.3 in Seattle; that of those working in the machine trades from 2.3 in Mt. Vernon to 14.1 in Bridgeport. It is interesting, on the other hand, to note the constancy of the representation of managerial service, the percentage ranging merely from 16.3 in St. Louis to 17.1 in Bridgeport, a range of less than 1 per cent. The differences in the character of the high-school population are to be explained either in terms of the special occupational and industrial interests of the four cities or in terms of the proportion of children of high-school age enrolled in the high school. For example, the first explanation accounts for the very large proportion of students in the Bridgeport High School whose fathers are engaged in the machine trades. Because of the nature of Bridgeport's industries an exceptionally large number of her workers are machinists. Consequently the number of machinists' children in the high school is unusually large. As a matter of fact, there is evidence to indicate that the machinists of Seattle send a much larger percentage of their children to high school than do those of Bridgeport. The relatively large proportion of children in the Mt. Vernon High School coming from the non-labor groups is also to be explained in terms of the character of the adult population. As already pointed out, Mt. Vernon is largely a residential city for middle-class folk having business in New York City. Differences in occupational and industrial interests, however, do not account for the appreciably larger representation of the proprietors in the St. Louis than in the Seattle schools. The second explanation is pertinent here. In the adult population there is actually a larger proportion of proprietors in Seattle than in St. Louis.   But since the St. Louis schools attract a much smaller percentage of the children of high-school age, her high-school population is more highly selected, containing fewer children from the laboring classes and a larger proportion from the well-to-do groups. Many other interesting differences will be noted by the careful reader who examines the table.

A more concrete picture of the high-school population is presented in Table X, in which are given the probable occupations of the fathers or guardians of one hundred high-school students taken at random from the high-school populations of the four cities.   If all the students in these high schools should be transported to the same place, and if the reader, happening to arrive at that place, should make inquiry of the first one hundred young people encountered regarding the parental occupation, he would get a result not very different from that presented in this table.   The writer is of the opinion further that a similar sampling of the high-school populations of four other representative American cities would yield a corresponding result, because of the fundamental similarity of populations and conditions from city to city.   To be sure, the exact occupations here given would not all appear, although a surprisingly large number of them would, but the general impression conveyed would be about the same.   Thus, instead of a hotelkeeper there might be an additional grocer; among the professional people there might be several physicians, and no civil engineer or architect; and in the place of the painter there might appear a sheet-metal worker.   In constructing this table individual occupations were necessarily selected somewhat arbitrarily in a good many instances, since it was necessary to choose from several occupations, no one of which occurred as frequently as once among every one hundred high-school students.   For example, the occupation of railroad conductor, or that of street-car motorman might have been selected instead of that of locomotive engineer.   The merest glance through the table will show many more cases where the same method was necessarily followed and where the same criticism is pertinent.   The larger occupational divisions, however, would probably appear in any large and representative high-school population just about as they do here.

COMPARISON WITH THE ADULT POPULATION

The analysis of the high-school population just presented gives the impression that the laboring classes do not constitute the preponderant element in the public high school.   The reader also, in all probability, carries the impression from everyday experience that in the

TABLE X

PROBABLE OCCUPATIONS OF THE FATHERS OR GUARDIANS OF 100 HIGH-SCHOOL STUDENTS TAKEN AT RANDOM FROM THE HIGH-SCHOOL POPULATIONS OF BRIDGEPORT, MT. VERNON, ST. LOUIS, AND SEATTLE—ALL FOUR YEARS COMBINED

Banker	Cigar Merchant	Clothier	Druggist	Druggist	Dry-Goods Merchant	Fruit Merchant	Furniture Merchant	Grain Broker	Grocer
Grocer	Grocer	Hotel-Keeper	Manufacturer	Manufacturer	Manufacturer	Publisher	Restaurant-Keeper	Shoe Merchant	Undertaker
Wholesale Merchant	Architect	Civil Engineer	Clergyman	Dentist	Editor	Lawyer	Musician	Pharmacist	Physician
Teacher	Building Contractor	Building Contractor	Building Contractor	Factory Foreman	Factory Foreman	Factory Foreman	Factory Superintendent	Factory Superintendent	Labor-Union Official
Lumber Inspector	Manager Express Company	Manager Theater	Police Captain	Railroad Agent	Sales Manager	Superintendent Post-Office	Yard Foreman	Buyer	Commercial Traveler
Commercial Traveler	Insurance Agent	Insurance Agent	Real Estate Agent	Real Estate Agent	Salesman in Store	Salesman in Store	Salesman in Store	Accountant	Bookkeeper
Cashier	Postal Clerk	Railroad Clerk	Receiving Clerk	Farmer	Farmer	Gardener	Baker (Proprietor)	Barber (Proprietor)	Cobbler (Proprietor)
Tailor (Proprietor)	Cabinet-Maker	Carpenter	Carpenter	Electrician	Mason	Painter	Plasterer	Plumber	Auto-Mechanic
Blacksmith	Boiler-Maker	Machinist	Machinist	Molder	Stationary Engineer	Compositor	Baker	Cigar-Maker	Tailor
Weaver	Chauffeur	Driver	Locomotive Engineer	Street-Car Conductor	Switchman	City Fireman	Policeman	Janitor	Laborer

ordinary American city a -large proportion of the population, if not a majority, are manual laborers. An attempt will now be made to discover the relation between the representation of each of the occupational groups in the general population and its representation in the high school.

The problem is complicated somewhat because of the well-known fact that certain of the occupations are carried on in large measure by young people. This is true of the clerical occupations, for example, certain commerical occupations, many of the miscellaneous trades, common labor, and others. Obviously it would not do therefore to compare the number of children in high school from a certain occupational group with the total number of persons engaged in that set of occupations. The occupation recruiting its ranks largely from persons on the youthful side of middle life could not possibly have a large proportion of children of high-school age. In attacking the problem two things are necessary: first, a knowledge of the age of the fathers of high-school students; and second, a knowledge of the number of men of this age to be found in each group of occupations.

The first of these two tasks is an easy one. It would not be difficult to make a rough estimate of the probable age-distribution of the fathers of high-school students from our knowledge of biological laws. It is not necessary to rely on such an *a priori* judgment, however, since the facts were obtained from the entire student population of one of the large Seattle high schools. Table XI is derived from the data furnished by these students. According to these figures an age-period of twenty years, the period from 40 to 60, includes over 80 per cent of the fathers; and the median age is 48.5 years. Since this particular high school draws its student body from no special social class, facts from other communities would probably parallel these rather closely.

TABLE XI

PROBABLE AGE-DISTRIBUTION OF THE FATHERS OF 1,000 HIGH-SCHOOL STUDENTS DERIVED FROM DATA GIVEN BY 1,391 STUDENTS IN LINCOLN HIGH SCHOOL, SEATTLE

Age-Period	30-4	35-9	40-4	45-9	50-4	55-9	60-4	65-9	70-4	75-9	Total	Median
Number.........	7	83	218	278	229	102	59	17	5	2	1,000	48.5

The second task, involving the determination of the number of men of the foregoing ages in these cities engaged in each set of occupations, is not so easy. In the first place, the occupational census for 1920 is not yet available. It is therefore necessary to place reliance on the data presented in the previous census, that of 1910. It is improbable, however, that the occupational distribution of the population in any city has changed in any marked degree during the past ten years. Consequently this may not be regarded as a source of serious error.

In the second place the age-periods recognized in the occupational census are not exactly the periods that would be most serviceable for this study. Furthermore, in the distribution of occupations by age-periods, the facts are not given for all occupations nor for all cities, but only for certain selected callings in each of the cities of more than 100,000 inhabitants. The only complete occupational census includes in a single figure the entire number of males over ten years of age pursuing each occupation. Thus for Bridgeport, St. Louis, and Seattle the number of males engaged in certain selected occupations is given by the following age-periods: ten to thirteen years; fourteen to fifteen; sixteen to twenty; twenty-one to forty-four; and forty-five years and over.

In view of these facts it was decided to merely make the best possible estimate of the number of males over forty-five years of age in each of the four cities engaged in each of the occupational divisions used in this study. This was done by first tabulating the total number of males over ten years of age to be found in each of these divisions in each of the four cities. Then, for each of the three larger cities, the selected occupations, for which the detailed age-distribution was given, were arranged under the classification used here, and the proportion of males over forty-five years of age was noted. The results of this calculation are given in Table XII. The wide range in the proportion of workers in the various occupations who are over forty-five years of age is at once apparent. At the one extreme are the managerial occupations in which 36 per cent of the workers are in this age-group; at the other are the clerical pursuits in which this percentage is but 14.

Perhaps the reader has already observed that two of the occupational divisions used in our classification do not appear in Table XII, namely, agricultural service and the artisan-proprietors. The first was not included because the agricultural occupations do not constitute a normal part of the life of the city. Many of the high-school students from this source are living in the city for the purpose of attending school. There is consequently no natural relation between the number of children in the high school whose fathers are engaged in these occupations and the number of adults so engaged, according to the census. The artisan-proprietors were omitted from this table, because in the census report they are not distinguished from the retail dealers and the manufacturers on the one hand and the artisans on the other.

TABLE XII

PERCENTAGE OF MALES ENGAGED IN EACH OCCUPATION WHO ARE
FORTY-FIVE YEARS OF AGE AND OVER, DERIVED FROM THE
CENSUS FIGURES FOR SELECTED OCCUPATIONS IN BRIDGEPORT,
ST. LOUIS, AND SEATTLE (1910)

Occupation	Percentage Forty-five Years or Over
Proprietors..................................	35
Professional service	28
Managerial service..........................	36
Commercial service	19
Clerical service	14
Building trades	27
Machine trades	24
Printing trades	16
Miscellaneous trades	17
Transportation service	17
Public service	30
Personal service	18
Miners, lumber-workers, fishermen	20
Common labor	20

Going back now to the total number of males over ten years of age engaged in each set of occupations in the four cities and applying the percentages given in Table XII, it is possible to approximate the actual number of men over forty-five to be found in these pursuits in 1910. This figure, along with the number of high-school students whose fathers or guardians are engaged in the same occupations, is given in Table XIII. The relation between these two sets of figures is also given in this table in terms of the number of students in the high schools of these four cities from each occupational group for every 1,000 men over forty-five engaged in the same occupations. This relation is really the final object of this rather extended series of computations and calculations.

This table shows very clearly that certain of the occupational groups have a much better representation in the high school than others in proportion to their representation in that part of our population in which the fathers of children of high-school age are found. Since these same facts are presented graphically in Figure 2, the reader's time will be economized by directing his attention to it at once. A hasty survey of the diagram shows that the laboring groups suffer in the comparison,

TABLE XIII

Estimated Number of Men Forty-five Years of Age and Over Engaged in Each Set of Occupations in Bridgeport, Mt. Vernon, St. Louis, and Seattle (1910); Number of High-School Students Whose Fathers or Guardians Are Engaged in Each Set of Occupations in the Same Cities, According to Studies Made in 1919–20 and 1920–21; and Number of the Latter for Every 1,000 of the Former for Each Set of Occupations

Parental Occupation	Men Forty-five Years of Age and Over	Students in High School	Number in High School for Every 1,000 Men Forty-five Years and Over
Proprietors	11,135	3,799	341
Professional service	4,520	1,629	360
Managerial service	7,120	2,846	400
Commercial service	6,682	1,637	245
Clerical service	4,558	996	219
Building trades	9,872	1,433	145
Machine trades	7,681	1,300	169
Printing trades	845	186	220
Miscellaneous trades	7,881	809	103
Transportation service	5,793	850	157
Public service	1,560	270	173
Personal service	4,941	249	50
Miners, lumber-workers, and fishermen	1,142	66	58
Common labor	12,429	213	17
Total	86,159	16,283	189

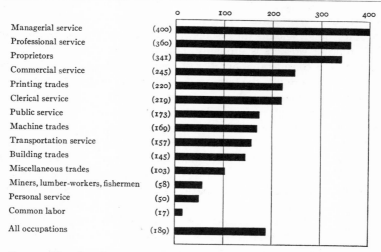

Fig. 2.—Showing the number of children in the high schools of four cities (Bridgeport, Mt. Vernon, St. Louis, Seattle) from each occupational group for every 1,000 males over forty-five years of age engaged in that occupation in the four cities, according to the Federal Census for 1910. Data from 16,283 high-school students.

and some of them suffer very badly.   Note the two extremes, for example.
Managerial service leads with 400 students in high school to every 1,000
men over forty-five in the general population.   At the other end of the
series is common labor with but seventeen.   The one labor group that
stands out with a good record is the printing trades.   It is one point ahead
of one of the non-labor groups, clerical service.   This is probably to be
explained in terms of the superior education of persons engaged in the
printing industry, the associations formed in the occupation, and the
stability of employment.   The favorable position of the public service
is probably to be explained in the same way.

A word of criticism is pertinent here.   In the light of other findings
of the study to be presented in later chapters there is reason to believe
that the order of the groups at the upper end of the diagram is not
altogether correct, due to certain difficulties arising from the effort to
translate the classification of the census over into the classification used
in this study.   The managerial service certainly should not rank
first, but it gets that rank here because the census does not in all cases
draw a clear line between managers and owners.   Also there are probably
a considerable number of individuals returned as commercial workers
who occupy managerial positions in commerce.   Consequently the
number of persons in the directing occupations is reported as somewhat
smaller than the actual facts would warrant.   This results in a larger
proportionate representation in high school.   Commercial service, on
the other hand, should rank somewhat higher than it is placed here.
This group of workers is probably diluted in the census report by the
inclusion of a considerable number of clerical workers, due to the ambi-
guity in the meaning of the term *clerk*.   The order of the first four groups
should probably be as follows: professional service, proprietors, commercial service, and managerial service.   The evidence favoring this
order will be noted from time to time in this study.

It is probable, for three reasons, that the proportion of children in
high school from the laboring groups is somewhat smaller than this
diagram suggests.   In the first place, the acceptance of the number of
men over forty-five in each occupation as the basis for comparison gives
a certain advantage to those occupations in which the proportion of such
men is relatively small, because over 30 per cent of the fathers of high-
school students are under forty-five.   As a consequence, the occupations
engaging few men beyond this age are not given a representation in the
general population proportionate to the actual number of fathers of
high-school students to be found in them.   Since on the average the

laboring classes are recruited less from the older men than are the other groups, it is apparent that the procedure followed here favors them. Of course, among the non-labor groups, it is true that the clerical and commercial workers are likewise favored. In the second place, the average number of children per family among the manual laborers is somewhat larger than it is among the other classes of the population. This is especially true of the lower grades of labor. Therefore, if the children from these elements in the population were enrolled in the high school in proportionate numbers, their ratio to the number of adults of the parental age in the same population groups should be larger than that for children from other classes with a lower birth-rate. In the third place, earlier marriages and a higher marriage rate among the laboring classes than among the more well-to-do members of society work toward the same end. These considerations should incline us therefore toward a revision of Table IX and Figure 2 in the direction of larger rather than smaller differences between the two extremes.

CHAPTER VI

PARENTAL OCCUPATION AND PROGRESS THROUGH THE SCHOOL

In the previous chapter the character of the total high-school population has been under examination. The proportionately larger representation of the proprietors, professionals, managers, and commercial workers was noted. In this chapter the composition of the school population in the earlier years will be compared with that in the later years. For this analysis we have data from the students in each of the four years in the high schools of the four cities and from the pupils of the sixth grade in Mt. Vernon.

THE FRESHMAN AND SENIOR YEARS

All are familiar with the fact that the number of students in the Senior year of the high school is but a small fraction of the total high-school enrolment, far below the 25 per cent that would result if the same number of young people entered the Freshman class every year, if all were promoted regularly, if there were no deaths or eliminations, and if there were no accretions except at the beginning of the first year. According to the report of the Bureau of Education for 1917–18, the students in the first year of the high school constituted 39.8 per cent of the total high-school enrolment in the United States; those in the second year, 26.9 per cent; those in the third year 18.8 per cent; and those in the fourth year but 14.5 per cent. The relatively small proportion in the last year of the high school is due chiefly to two causes, namely, elimination and the increasing size of the Freshman class, the latter resulting from the normal population increase and the increasing interest in secondary education on the part of children and their parents.

Because of the small number of students in the Senior year it is naturally assumed that some sort of selection is going on continually in the high school. Many studies have been made of the process of elimination and of the character of the eliminated. It is our purpose here to note the social composition of the student population in the last year as contrasted with the first. The facts for the four cities combined appear in Table XIV. For each of the two years the percentages of students coming from the various occupational groups are given. It is plain that the Senior class in these high schools does not differ from the Freshman class merely in the age of its students and their advancement in the course.   The proportions coming from the different elements in the population are noticeably different.   The children from the laboring classes constitute in every instance a smaller percentage of the total enrolment of the last than of the first year of the school.   On the other hand a larger percentage of the Seniors than of the Freshmen are children of the proprietors, the professionals, the managers, and the commercial workers.   Two groups make equal proportionate contributions to the two classes, namely, the clerical and agricultural workers.

TABLE XIV

PERCENTAGE OF STUDENTS IN EACH OF TWO HIGH-SCHOOL YEARS FROM EACH OF THE OCCUPATIONAL GROUPS IN THE HIGH SCHOOLS OF BRIDGEPORT, MT. VERNON, ST. LOUIS, AND SEATTLE: DATA FROM 6,782 FRESHMEN AND 2,522 SENIORS

Parental Occupation	Freshman	Senior
Proprietors	17.7	22.9
Professional service	7.7	12.5
Managerial service	15.4	19.1
Commercial service	8.6	11.1
Clerical service	5.9	5.9
Agricultural service	2.3	2.3
Artisan-proprietors	4.4	3.5
Building trades	8.8	5.3
Machine trades	8.3	4.6
Printing trades	1.0	.8
Miscellaneous trades	4.8	2.3
Transportation service	6.2	3.6
Public service	1.7	1.1
Personal service	1.4	.9
Miners, lumber-workers, fishermen	.5	.3
Common labor	1.8	.6
Unknown	3.5	3.2
Total	100.0	100.0

These same facts under a slight adaptation are presented graphically in Figure 3.   Here is shown for each group the number in the Senior year for every 100 from the same group in the Freshman year.   This ratio that the one year bears toward the other exhibits a very wide range among the various occupations, as an inspection of the diagram clearly reveals.   As a general proposition, those occupations having a relatively poor representation in the high school are just the ones with a small proportion in the Senior year.   At the two extremes are professional service and common labor. For the former there are 60.2 students in the Senior year for every 100 in the Freshman year of the high school; whereas, for the latter this ratio is but 12.4. The facts for the Sophomore and Junior years, as might be assumed, show a condition intermediate between the two extreme years. They are therefore not given here. It seems that as we pass from year to year in the high school, we see the children from the laboring classes constituting a less and less important element of the student population.

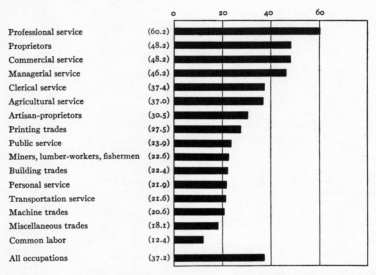

FIG. 3.—Showing for each occupational group the number of students in the Senior year for every 100 in the Freshman year of the high school. Data from Bridgeport, Mt. Vernon, St. Louis, and Seattle.

An analysis of the data from the different cities shows some differences, but they are quantitative rather than qualitative. The laboring classes hold their own better in some of the cities than they do in others, but in every instance their record is relatively inferior to that of the other groups. Thus the nine laboring groups (the building trades, machine trades, printing trades, miscellaneous trades, transportation service, public service, personal service, miners, lumber-workers, and fishermen, and common labor) contribute 26.5 per cent of the membership in the Senior class in Bridgeport; 23.3 per cent in Seattle; 15.2 per cent in St. Louis; and but 4.3 per cent in Mt. Vernon. These differences are, to be sure, accounted for in some measure by occupational differences in the populations of the several cities. The high proportion in Bridge-port is certainly largely explained in this way. Bridgeport is very highly industrialized. The laboring classes consequently constitute an exceptionally large element in the population. The very low percentage of children from these classes in the Senior year of Mt. Vernon is also to be explained largely in terms of the occupational character of the population itself. The records of Seattle and St. Louis, on the other hand, are not to be interpreted in this way. The large representation of the laboring groups in the former city is not due to their large numbers in the general population. As a matter of fact, they form a less important numerical group in Seattle than in St. Louis. The high schools of the former seem to hold the children of laborers unusually well.

THE SOCIAL COMPOSITION OF THE SIXTH GRADE

By the time the first year of the high school is reached the student population is already greatly reduced and presumably already considerably selected. It is fortunate therefore that for at least one of the cities, Mt. Vernon, facts regarding the social composition of the entire sixth grade were secured. Of course there are many children who do not even reach this point in our educational system, because of retardation and elimination. This group of children, therefore, may be assumed to be somewhat different socially from the children in the first grade, or from the children secured by taking a cross-section of the entire population at any particular age. It nevertheless provides us with significant data for comparative purposes.

The percentage of children from each of the occupational groups for both the sixth grade and the Senior year of the high school is given in Table XV. The difference between the first and last high-school years already noted is seen to be greatly accentuated. And it is probable that the difference would be somewhat greater in a city with a larger laboring population. Even here the majority of the children in the sixth grade come from the homes of laborers. This is certainly not true of the students in the Senior year of the high school. These two cross-sections of the school population give us two very different sociological pictures. They might almost be conceived as representative of two different social orders.

The contrast is so striking that it seems advisable to give it a graphical representation. This is done in Figure 4 by taking four occupational groups showing different tendencies and plotting a curve for each, picturing its percentage representation in the school population of each

TABLE XV

PERCENTAGE OF CHILDREN FROM EACH OCCUPATIONAL GROUP IN EACH OF TWO
SCHOOL GRADES. DATA FROM 739 CHILDREN IN THE SIXTH GRADE AND
136 IN THE SENIOR YEAR OF THE HIGH SCHOOL, MT. VERNON

Parental Occupation	Sixth Grade	Senior Year of High School
Proprietors...........................	13.1	29.4
Professional service....................	6.8	16.9
Managerial service.....................	10.0	20.6
Commercial service....................	6.0	15.4
Clerical service.......................	4.3	5.2
Agricultural service...................	2.3	.0
Artisan-proprietors....................	9.1	5.2
Building trades.......................	16.5	.7
Machine trades.......................	4.7	.7
Printing trades.......................	.4	.0
Miscellaneous trades..................	5.2	2.2
Transportation service.................	4.2	.7
Public service........................	1.5	.0
Personal service......................	2.4	.0
Miners, lumber-workers, fishermen.......	.4	.0
Common labor........................	10.8	.0
Unknown............................	2.3	3.0
Total...........................	100.0	100.0

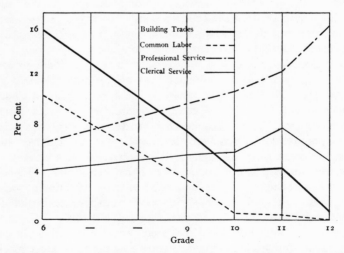

FIG. 4.—Showing percentage of children in each grade from the sixth to the
twelfth whose fathers are engaged in each of four groups of occupations.   Mt. Vernon,
May, 1921.   No data for seventh and eighth grades.

grade from the sixth to the twelfth. Since we have no data from the seventh and eighth grades the position of the curve in these grades for each group is purely hypothetical. Based on actual facts it would probably not follow exactly the course given it here, but its general direction would be the same. The diagram shows in an impressive way the diverse reactions of these four groups to educational opportunity. Each of the occupational divisions was chosen for a reason—common labor and professional service, because they represent the two extremes; clerical service because it represents an intermediate tendency; and the building trades because they constitute the largest labor group as well as the largest occupational group in the sixth grade. The proportion of children from the building trades and common labor in each grade diminishes very rapidly as we pass from one year to the next. The latter has practically disappeared in the Sophomore year, and the former are barely able to keep a slight representation until the end of the high school. Professional service, on the other hand, furnishes a constantly increasing percentage of the school population as progress is made through the schools. Clerical service improves its position slightly, but does little more than hold its own. The other non-labor groups show tendencies similar to those of professional service, and the remaining labor groups behave much as the building trades.

Perhaps one more chart bearing on this same matter will not tire the reader. In Figure 5 is shown for each occupational group the number of children in the Senior year of the high school for every one hundred in the sixth grade. Comment is hardly necessary. The diagram carries its own message. It brings out with peculiar force the enormous contrast between the school populations in these two years of the Mt. Vernon public schools.

Since the organization of most of the work in most of our high schools assumes four years of attendance, the number and character of the student population in the Senior year might be expected to afford one of the most satisfactory measures of the extension of secondary educational opportunity. The Senior class should tell much about the success of the high school in reaching the various elements in the population. It is for this group especially that the ordinary high school is maintained.

In the previous chapter the total high-school population was analyzed in the light of the social composition of that adult population from which children of high-school age come. This same thing is done for the students of the Senior year in Figure 6. Here is shown for each occupational group the number of students in the Senior year of the

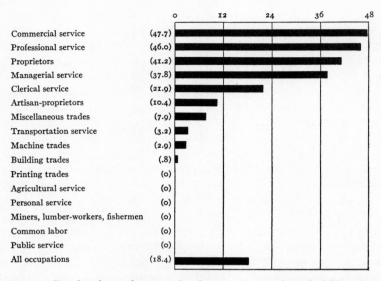

FIG. 5.—Showing for each occupational group the number of children in the Senior year of the high school for every 100 from the same group in the sixth grade of the elementary school.   Mt. Vernon, May, 1921.

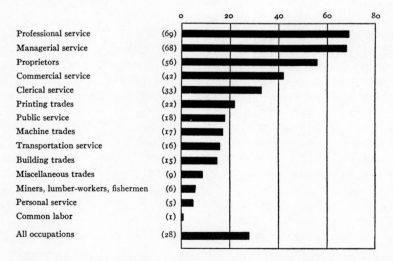

FIG. 6.—Showing the number of children in the Senior year of the high school in four cities (Bridgeport, Mt. Vernon, St. Louis, Seattle) from each occupational group for every 1,000 males over forty-five years of age engaged in that occupation in the four cities, according to the Federal Census for 1910.   Data from 2,382 high-school Seniors.

high school in the four cities for every 1,000 men over forty-five years of age engaged in that occupation in these same cities, according to the thirteenth census.   The reasons for choosing the number of males over forty-five as the basis for comparison have already been given, so need not be repeated.   As might be expected from the data presented in this chapter thus far, the differences between the laboring and the non-laboring groups are greater here than for the total high-school population. It appears that the chances that the child of a father engaged in one of the professional pursuits will reach the Senior year of the high school are sixty-nine times as great as those of the child whose father is a common laborer.   These two occupational classes represent the extremes. The others fall in between in a gradual series with the laboring groups at the lower end of the distribution.

Table XVI gives a concrete picture of the occupations represented in the Senior year of the high school as Table XI did for the entire high school.   The same caution is necessary in interpreting this as was suggested in the discussion of the earlier table.   Many of these particular occupations might not appear in a group of one hundred students selected at random from the Senior classes in the high schools of these four cities, but the larger groups of which these occupations are representative would.   Nothing could show more plainly than this table that the students in the Senior year of the public high school are socially a highly selected group.

The objection may be raised here that the differences between the earlier and later years are due to the promotion of the fathers from less responsible to more responsible positions, or to their acquisition of property which enables them to set up business for themselves and thus enter the ranks of the proprietors.   Obviously to the extent that this is going on during the period of high-school attendance the character of the student population in the Senior year will differ from that of the students in the Freshman year in the direction indicated in this chapter. If, for example, a goodly proportion of the fathers of high-school Freshmen who are engaged in manual labor are promoted to managerial positions or go into business for themselves as proprietors during the succeeding three years, the students in the Senior year whose fathers are engaged in the managerial occupations or as proprietors will show an increased proportion, even though there is no elimination whatsoever from high school in the meantime.   It must be assumed of course at the same time that an equal number of fathers are not demoted from managerial positions or do not lose property, making it necessary for them to fall back into the ranks of labor.

TABLE XVI

PROBABLE OCCUPATIONS OF THE FATHERS OR GUARDIANS OF 100 HIGH-SCHOOL SENIORS TAKEN AT RANDOM FROM THE HIGH-SCHOOL POPULATIONS OF BRIDGEPORT, MT. VERNON, ST. LOUIS, AND SEATTLE

Banker	Cigar Merchant	Clothier	Clothier	Druggist	Druggist	Dry-Goods Merchant	Fruit Merchant	Furniture Merchant	Grain Broker
Grocer	Grocer	Grocer	Grocer	Hotel-Keeper	Manufacturer	Manufacturer	Manufacturer	Manufacturer	Publisher
Restaurant-Keeper	Shoe Merchant	Undertaker	Wholesale Merchant	Architect	Artist	Chemist	Civil Engineer	Clergyman	Dentist
Editor	Lawyer	Musician	Pharmacist	Physician	Surgeon	Teacher	Building Contractor	Building Contractor	Building Contractor
Factory Foreman	Factory Foreman	Factory Foreman	Factory Superintendent	Factory Superintendent	Insurance Official	Labor-Union Official	Lumber Inspector	Manager of Express Company	Manager of Grocery Store
Manager of Theater	Police Captain	Promoter	Railroad Agent	Sales Manager	Superintendent Post-Office	Yard Foreman	Buyer	Commercial Traveler	Commercial Traveler
Insurance Agent	Insurance Agent	Real Estate Agent	Real Estate Agent	Real Estate Agent	Salesman in Store	Salesman in Store	Salesman in Store	Salesman in Store	Accountant
Bookkeeper	Cashier	Postal Clerk	Railroad Clerk	Receiving Clerk	Farmer	Gardener	Baker (Proprietor)	Barber (Proprietor)	Cobbler (Proprietor)
Tailor (Proprietor)	Carpenter	Electrician	Mason	Painter	Plumber	Auto-Mechanic	Machinist	Machinist	Molder
Stationary Engineer	Compositor	Baker	Tailor	Chauffeur	Driver	Locomotive Engineer	Street-Car Conductor	Policeman	Janitor

Fortunately we have at hand the facts bearing on this question. For the purpose of securing information indicating the degree and nature of the change of occupation on the part of parents during the period of high-school attendance this question was asked the students in the St. Louis high schools: "What was your father's occupation three years ago?" The period of three years instead of four formed the basis of this question, because at any particular moment, such as the time when our study was made, the number of years between the Freshman and the Senior class is exactly three. A tabulation of the facts for the Senior year shows that during the three preceding years the fathers of but nine students out of a total of 1,030 had advanced from the laboring occupations into those five groups of occupations styled as non-laboring in this study. During the same period the fathers of seven of these students passed in the other direction, from the non-laboring to the laboring classes. This leaves a difference of less than two-tenths of 1 per cent to account for the enormous differences already noted between the Freshman and Senior years. An examination of the clerical occupations also revealed no evidence that the proportion of this group in the several high-school years is modified by either promotion or demotion. But two clerical workers were promoted to managerial positions, and two were demoted to clerical positions from the managerial. It seems that the fathers of practically all high-school students have reached that point in years where no promotion may be expected to take them out of the occupational classes they have reached. At this time in life there is apparently but a small, a negligible chance, that a man will change his occupation sufficiently to take him from one of these groups to another. All of which goes to show that socially the student population in the Senior year of the high school is highly selected as compared with that of the Freshman year or the earlier grades.

CHAPTER VII

PARENTAL OCCUPATION AND CHILDREN OF HIGH-SCHOOL AGE NOT
IN HIGH SCHOOL

In order to throw additional light on this question of the selective
character of the high school, four groups of children of high-school age
not in high school were studied. Of these one was in Seattle and
three in Bridgeport. Their social character will now be examined.

CHILDREN OF HIGH-SCHOOL AGE AT WORK IN SEATTLE

Information regarding the occupations of the fathers or guardians
of 514 children of high-school age (fourteen to seventeen years inclusive)
at work in the commercial and industrial establishments of Seattle was
obtained in December of 1919. These facts were secured through
personal interviews with the children by field workers. The two sexes
were almost equally well represented, there being 249 girls and 265 boys.
Obviously this does not include all of the children of high-school age at
work or not in high school, but the number is large enough to be representative.

Percentage data from this investigation are presented in Table
XVII in which a comparison is made between this group of children of
high-school age at work and the total Seattle high-school population
for which the occupational data were obtained. The small group in
the high school classified as "unknown" in previous tables and diagrams
was not recognized in the computation of percentages here.

A glance at the table suffices to show the profound differences
between the two groups. The proprietors, professional service, managerial service, clerical service, agricultural service, artisan-proprietors,
and printing trades have better proportionate representation in the high
school than out. This is especially pronounced for the first four groups.
The favorable balance for the farmers and the clerical workers is not so
marked. The printing trades have the best record among the labor
groups, but the number of cases is so small that the conclusions drawn
should not be too rigid. The artisan-proprietors also make a very good
showing, but the returns on this group are so subject to error because of
insufficient data that the comparison certainly does not represent the
actual situation. On the other hand, the laboring groups, as a rule,

appear in a rather poor light.   Taken together and excluding the farmers they account for over 75 per cent of the children of high-school age at work.   Without doubt the poorest showing is that made by common labor, while the best seems to be that made by the proprietors.

TABLE XVII

PERCENTAGE DISTRIBUTION OF THE OCCUPATIONS OF THE FATHERS OR GUARDIANS OF TWO GROUPS OF CHILDREN. DATA FROM 514 CHILDREN OF HIGH-SCHOOL AGE AT WORK AND 6,138 CHILDREN IN HIGH SCHOOL, SEATTLE

Parental Occupation	Children of High-School Age at Work	Children in High School
Proprietors.........................	2.5	17.4
Professional service...................	4.1	11.4
Managerial service....................	8.2	17.1
Commercial service...................	2.7	8.7
Clerical service......................	3.5	4.6
Agricultural service...................	3.9	4.8
Artisan-proprietors...................	.2	2.6
Building trades......................	24.3	11.8
Machine trades......................	11.1	7.4
Printing trades......................	.2	1.1
Miscellaneous trades.................	5.8	2.0
Transportation service................	9.5	5.6
Public service.......................	2.5	1.5
Personal service.....................	1.8	1.6
Miners, lumber-workers, fishermen........	3.7	1.0
Common labor.......................	16.0	1.4
Total.........................	100.0	100.0

In Figure 7 this comparison between the children in high school and those outside is put in graphical form.   For each occupational group it shows the number of children among those at work for every one hundred from the same group attending high school.   It should be remembered, however, that data were secured from but 514 children at work which is only 8 per cent of the number studied in the high school.   This diagram speaks for itself in unmistakable terms.   The ratio ranges all the way from 93 for common labor to 1 for the proprietors.

Perhaps it is surprising to the reader that the managerial and professional occupations do have so large a representation outside the high school, and it was somewhat of a surprise to the writer.   It is due in part to the difficulties of occupational classification already referred to.   At best, there is a wide range in each of these groups.   The major portion of the managerial group was made up of foremen and people holding relatively low-grade positions.   The same may be said of the other group. The designation musician, for instance, has a rather wide range of meaning. Yet, it must be said, that among the professional occupations the clergymen had the largest representation. This may be accounted for in part on the grounds suggested above, since the prophetic gift, independent of a thorough and rigorous professional preparation, may be regarded as sufficient qualification for entry into

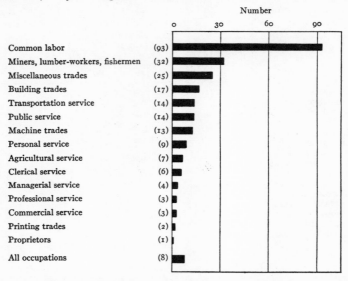

FIG. 7.—Showing the number of children from each occupational group among children of high-school age at work for every 100 children from the same group attending high school. Data from 6,387 children in high school and 514 at work. Seattle, 1919–20.

the ministry. There was evidence, however, to show that in this group were several boys who had run away from home. This sort of thing occurs in every one of the groups, as well as other serious misfortunes, such as separation of parents, invalidism or death of the father.

THE BRIDGEPORT EVENING HIGH SCHOOL

In Bridgeport three groups were studied, not exhaustively, but sufficiently to provide comparative data. As already stated, they were the evening high school, the state trade school, and the compulsory continuation classes, the latter being maintained in the evening for children from fourteen to sixteen years of age who have left school without having completed the elementary school.

The students in the evening high school constitute an interesting group, since, presumably, they are young persons desirous of further education who, because of some misfortune, are compelled to engage in gainful employment during the regular working-day. They are attending school during the hours which most young people use for recreation and entertainment. This speaks well for their moral qualities.

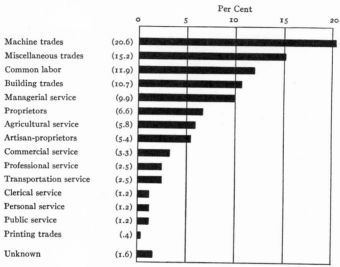

FIG. 8.—Showing by percentages the occupations of the fathers of 243 students attending the high-school department of the evening school. Bridgeport, December, 1920.

The enrolment in this school is approximately one thousand. It is a somewhat heterogeneous group, including a few students who are high-school graduates as well as great numbers of persons well beyond the high-school age. They are registered not only in the high-school department, which provides a sequence and variety of courses comparable to the course of study of the regular day high school, but also in special courses and subjects of considerable diversity. The 243 students whose records are used in this study were enrolled in the high-school department, were not high-school graduates, and were all twenty-one years of age or under. Of these 147 were girls and 96 were boys. The median age of the girls was 17.9; that of the boys, 18.6; and that of the two sexes combined, 18.2. Thus we have a group, slightly older than the regular high-school population, yet comparable to it in most respects.

Figure 8 shows the occupational distribution of the fathers of these 243 young people. It will be observed that the four leading groups are labor groups, with common labor occupying the third place. A re-examination of Table IX, portraying the social composition of the population of the day high school, is of interest here. It is clear that the two populations are very different. In the high school the proprietors and the managerial occupations are in first and second places, whereas in the evening high school they hold sixth and fifth places respectively. This excellent representation of certain of the labor groups apparently indicates the existence of many young people among them who are ambitious for larger educational opportunities.

THE STATE TRADE SCHOOL AT BRIDGEPORT

The trade school at Bridgeport is supported and administered by the state of Connecticut under the provisions of the Smith-Hughes Act. Its purpose is therefore intensely practical and it aims to turn out efficient workmen with only as much theory as is necessary to serve this purpose. It does this by providing a 4,800-hour course in each of fifteen trades, covering a period of two years and organized on the regular eight-hour basis now common in industry. There is no official connection with the city schools, although recently there has been inaugurated a co-operative course in industrial arts in which the academic training is given in the city high school and the trade training in the trade school. But it should be borne in mind that this school points very definitely into industry and those who enter it have renounced all intention of pursuing a higher education.

The school has a registration of approximately 400 students of which the great majority are boys. The information card was filled out by 198 students of whom 129 were in the first year and 69 in the second; 14 were girls and 184 were boys. The returns were not complete because many of the boys were only half-time students and others were out on project work. Then, too, a portion of the enrolment was composed of soldiers who were far beyond the high-school age. Records from this group were not wanted. However, there is no reason for believing that the group studied is not representative of the trade-school population generally.

Figure 9 shows the occupational distribution of the fathers of these 198 students. The same four great labor groups lead here as in the evening high school, except that common labor has forged ahead of the miscellaneous trades. On the whole, the labor groups are somewhat better represented in the trade school than in the evening high school, while it naturally follows that the reverse is true for the non-labor groups. And a comparison of the trade school with the regular day high school shows two markedly different groups of children from the standpoint of the population sources from which they come. As a matter of fact, 54.7 per cent of the students in the high school come from the five non-labor groups (proprietors, professional, managerial, commercial, and

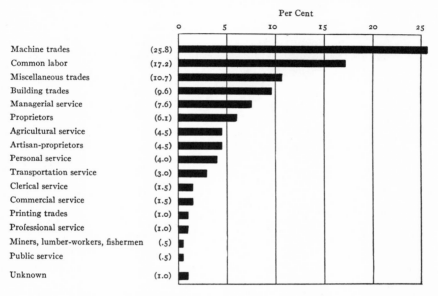

Per Cent

		0	5	10	15	20	25
Machine trades	(25.8)						
Common labor	(17.2)						
Miscellaneous trades	(10.7)						
Building trades	(9.6)						
Managerial service	(7.6)						
Proprietors	(6.1)						
Agricultural service	(4.5)						
Artisan-proprietors	(4.5)						
Personal service	(4.0)						
Transportation service	(3.0)						
Clerical service	(1.5)						
Commercial service	(1.5)						
Printing trades	(1.0)						
Professional service	(1.0)						
Miners, lumber-workers, fishermen	(.5)						
Public service	(.5)						
Unknown	(1.0)						

FIG. 9.—Showing by percentages the occupations of the fathers of 198 students in the state trade school. Bridgeport, February, 1921.

clerical occupations), while but 17.7 per cent of the trade-school students come from these same five occupational classes.

THE COMPULSORY CONTINUATION CLASSES OF BRIDGEPORT

In the compulsory continuation classes of the Bridgeport evening school is found a most interesting group of children for the student of education. Many of the "problems" of elementary education are found in these classes. As already intimated, Connecticut has a state law that compels children from fourteen to sixteen years of age who have left school without completing the grades, to attend these evening classes until they either reach their sixteenth birthday or complete the eighth grade. There are consequently gathered into these classes great numbers of children unfortunate either by nature or by nurture. Here are the misfits, the children who cannot "get on" in the elementary school, those who have been educationally discouraged, those whose schooling has been interrupted in one way or another, children whose homes lack the educational stimulus, children who have no homes. About these children one thing is certain. It is this: Practically none of them will ever attend high school. They are a sampling of that great group of children still to be found in our cities and towns for whom the high school simply does not exist. At best, it is nothing more than a name to them. And it is for this reason particularly that they are introduced into this study.

There are probably about a thousand children enrolled in these classes which meet at those school buildings which are conveniently located. But the attendance is very irregular and the composition of the classes is continually changing because of the admission of new recruits from the elementary school and the mustering out of individual after individual following the sixteenth birthday. It should be pointed out, however, that a significant number do remain after they reach this age.

Sociological data were obtained from 579 children in these classes, 305 girls and 274 boys, which included practically all those in attendance on the evening the cards were passed out. As might be expected, many of the cards were incompletely filled out. Where the information missing was important the cards were sent back and the facts especially desired were secured in this way in most cases. The final result is fairly satisfactory for purposes of this study.

Figure 10 gives a good picture of the social composition of this group of children. The representation of the five non-labor groups has shrunk to 10.3 per cent, and over half of these are found in the managerial service alone. Most of them are labor foremen. The fathers of more than one-fourth (26.6) of the 579 children are common laborers, whereas but 1.7 per cent of the children in the high school come from this occupational group.

What amounts to a summary of the situation found in Bridgeport is given in Figure 11. Here a comparison is drawn between the high-school population, on the one hand, and these three groups of non-high-school children combined, on the other. The bars represent for each occupational class the number of children in the latter for every one hundred in the former. The tremendous difference between common labor and all

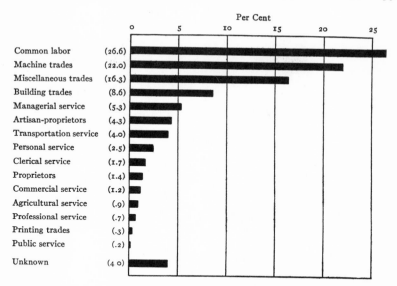

FIG. 10.—Showing by percentages the occupations of the fathers of 579 children attending the compulsory continuation classes of the evening school. Bridgeport, December, 1920.

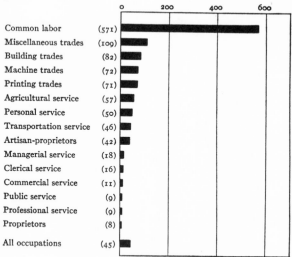

FIG. 11.—Showing the number of children from each occupational group among children of high-school age not in high school (evening high school, trade school, and compulsory continuation classes) for every 100 students from the same group attending the regular day high school. Data from 2,257 children in high school and 1,020 in the other three groups. Bridgeport, 1920–21.

the other groups is striking.   As a matter of fact, all the labor groups occupy relatively unfavorable positions, except the workers in public service, who are found in third place.   Too much weight, however, should not be attached to this exception because of the small number of cases involved.

In concluding this chapter, the reader's attention should be called to the similarity of the results obtained in Seattle and Bridgeport.   It is clear that these groups of children of high-school age outside the regular high school are very different in social composition from the high-school population itself.   The several occupational groups apparently arrange themselves in a graded series, with the proprietors and professional service at one end, and common labor at the other.

CHAPTER VIII

PARENTAL OCCUPATION AND THE COURSE OF STUDY

In response to the growing social demand for an enriched course of study the public high school has made many curriculum changes, particularly since the opening of the twentieth century. Among them is the organization of several curricula, each designed to meet the needs of some portion of the high-school population. Those who have been strong advocates of these adjustments have maintained that the single curriculum, pointing toward the higher education, is inadequate and involves an injustice to great masses of young people who cannot possibly go on to college. It will be interesting to see how children coming from the various occupational groups react to this complex program.

In each of the cities studied several different curricula are offered the students in its high schools. If all four cities offered the same curricula, it would be possible and desirable to discuss these curricula *seriatim*, bringing to bear on each curriculum the facts from all the cities. But such is not the case. Each city has organized its high-school course of study to suit itself, within certain limitations set by college-entrance requirements. Consequently the relation between parental occupation and course of study will be studied in each of the cities separately.

BRIDGEPORT

In the Bridgeport High School six curricula are offered the students. These are the college preparatory, scientific, general, normal, commercial, and industrial arts courses. Since the normal course is exclusively for girls and the industrial arts strictly for boys, this means five curricula for each sex. As will be noted later, however, several of these courses receive very light patronage.

Space will not permit a detailed description of each curriculum, and perhaps such a description is quite unnecessary, since the general content of most of them is familiar to anyone acquainted with the American public high school. The following brief characterization taken from the high-school circular to parents will have to suffice.

I. *The college preparatory course* prepares for the best colleges and universities as well as for the law and medical preparatory courses.

It stresses the traditional academic subjects with special emphasis on the languages.

II. *The scientific preparatory course* prepares for the best scientific and technical schools in the country. It differs from the college preparatory course merely in a larger provision for the study of science and mathematics at the expense of the languages.

III. *The general course* is designed to offer a broad and practical education to those who are not preparing for a college or a scientific school. Subject to the approval of the principal, the student is allowed extensive privileges of election.

IV. *The normal course* prepares students for the city normal school and offers a well-rounded and practical course with definite requirements for girls who are preparing for the important work of teaching.

V. *The commercial course* prepares rather definitely for clerical positions with the usual offerings in the special subjects.

VI. *The industrial arts course* is conducted through co-operation with the state trade school in which the shopwork is given. The course is either three or four years in length and is intended to train for the manufacturing and mechanical trades.

TABLE XVIII

SELECTION OF CURRICULA BY CHILDREN FROM THE VARIOUS OCCUPATIONAL GROUPS, BRIDGEPORT HIGH SCHOOL, ALL CLASSES

PARENTAL OCCUPATION	GIRLS						BOYS					
	College	Normal	Commercial	General	Scientific	Total	College	Industrial	Commercial	General	Scientific	Total
Proprietors.................	88	57	81	1	2	229	105	4	20	6	87	222
Professional service........	40	11	17	2	.....	70	25	2	2	1	37	67
Managerial service	39	74	92	6	.....	211	36	12	19	12	95	174
Commercial service........	26	18	36	2	.....	82	31	1	15	1	33	81
Clerical service............	11	16	33	3	.....	63	10	1	8	.....	16	35
Agricultural service........	7	8	15	2	.....	32	1	3	5	3	5	17
Artisan-proprietors	5	16	42	.....	.....	63	21	1	5	1	20	48
Building trades	3	19	37	1	.....	60	15	2	9	2	28	56
Machine trades	8	45	111	4	.....	168	41	10	24	6	69	150
Printing trades	1	.....	2	.....	.....	3	2	.....	1	.....	1	4
Miscellaneous trades	6	23	51	1	1	82	26	4	6	2	19	57
Transportation service	2	14	23	.....	.....	39	12	1	9	2	14	38
Public service.............	5	10	21	.....	.....	36	5	.....	7	1	8	21
Personal service...........	1	6	20	.....	.....	27	5	1	6	1	12	25
Common labor	.....	2	14	.....	.....	16	4	2	9	1	6	22
Unknown.................	8	13	18	.....	.....	39	4	3	3	.....	10	20
Total...............	250	332	613	22	3	1,220	343	47	148	39	460	1,037

An examination of Table XVIII shows very few girls taking either the general or the scientific curriculum. Likewise, the number of boys in either the general or industrial arts course is small.   This leaves but three courses each for the boys and girls.

The table reveals no pronounced tendency for the selection of courses among the boys to fall along occupational lines.   Each of the three courses has a fairly good representation from all of the larger groups.   It should be remembered, however, that so far as outlook is concerned, there is but little difference between the college and the scientific curricula.

Among the girls, on the other hand, a very different situation is found.   The girls from the several occupational groups do show tendencies

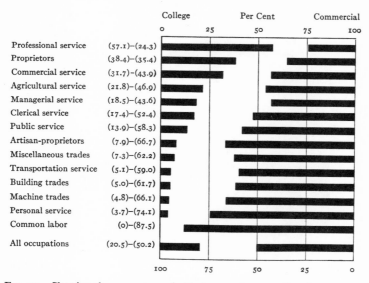

FIG. 12.—Showing the percentage of girls from each occupational group pursuing the college preparatory and commercial curricula, Bridgeport High School.

to gravitate toward certain courses.   This is clearly brought out in Figure 12 and Figure 13.   In the former the percentage of students from each of these groups taking the college preparatory course is compared with the percentage in the commercial course.   At the one extreme are the girls whose fathers are engaged in the professional occupations, with 57.1 per cent in the college course and but 24.3 per cent in the commercial.   At the other is the common labor group with not a single girl in the former course and 87.5 per cent in the latter.

In Figure 13 the social composition of the entire group of girls pursuing the college preparatory curriculum in all four years is given. It shows in a striking way the class-character of this course. The first five groups, which may be regarded as the strictly non-labor groups, include 81.6 per cent of the total. Of the remaining 18.4 per cent, 2.8 are from the agricultural occupations; 2.0 from the artisan-proprietors; and 3.2 from fathers of unknown occupation. There remain but 10.4 per cent of these girls to represent the manual-labor groups. This

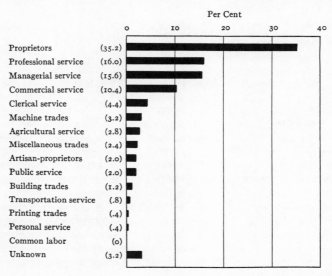

FIG. 13.—Showing by percentages the occupations of the fathers of the 250 girls pursuing the college preparatory course in the Bridgeport High School.

tendency is yet more pronounced in the Senior year where 88.1 per cent come from the five non-labor groups and but 2.4 per cent from the labor groups.

MT. VERNON

On a small scale Mt. Vernon is experimenting with the specialized high school. There are two separate school buildings. In the one, known as the Academic High School, are taught the classical, scientific, and general curricula; while in the other, a vocational school, the commercial and practical arts curricula are offered. The situation here is of especial interest to us because in the other three cities studied the high school is of the general type. Exception might be taken to this statement in its application to Bridgeport, for, although there is but one high school supported by the city, the state of Connecticut maintains a trade school there that enrols children of high-school age. It might, therefore, be maintained that in this city there are really two secondary schools, in one of which are taught the academic subjects; in the other, the practical arts.

In all, six curricula are offered, five for the boys and five for the girls. Of these, three are academic and three vocational. To the former belong the classical, scientific, and general; and to the latter, the commercial, industrial arts, and household arts courses. The vocational curricula are so organized as to make possible the granting of certificates for short units of work. A short description of each course follows.

I. *The classical course* is designed to meet the entrance requirements of college courses leading to the degree of Bachelor of Arts. Its distinctive feature is the requirement of three years of Latin and three years of either Greek, French, or Spanish.

II. *The scientific course* prepares for college courses leading to the degree of Bachelor of Science, as well as for engineering and technical schools. It consists of about equal parts of English, foreign languages, mathematics, and science.

III. *The general course* is rather elastic in its provisions and is organized to meet the needs of two classes of students: (1) those intending to enter a normal or training-school for teachers; and (2) those who will leave school at the end of the high-school course. The subjects, however, are all from the traditional academic offering.

IV. *The commercial course* includes the usual clerical and commercial branches, English, a little science and mathematics, and some provision for electives. It points toward wage-earning in the clerical occupations.

V. *The industrial arts course* prepares in a general way for industrial pursuits. It is organized under a liberal elective system with the single restriction that seven-twelfths of the time be given to subjects of an academic character and the remainder to industrial branches, including joinery and wood-turning, printing, machine-shop practice, etc.

VI. *The household arts course*, pointing toward homemaking, is organized according to the same principles as the course immediately preceding.

Facts showing the selection of curricula by the students from the various occupational groups are presented in Table XIX. Because of the small number of cases representing certain of the occupations, the data for the boys and girls are combined in a single table. For a similar reason the industrial arts and household arts curricula are brought together under the more general caption of "practical arts." This table gives for each occupational group the actual number and the percentage of students pursuing each of the curricula. It is interesting to note the great popularity of the classical course. Each of the curricula is well patronized except the practical arts course.

An examination of that half of the table giving the percentage of students from each group enrolled in each curriculum reveals tendencies of the order already noted in Bridgeport. If we take any one of the curricula we find a wide range in the emphasis given to it by children from the different occupations. Of course, in making these observations, too much weight should not be attached to the distribution for the occupations represented by very small numbers of students, such as the printing trades, personal service, public service, and the miners, lumber-workers, and fishermen. The curricula presenting the widest range are the classical and commercial courses. Fifty-eight per cent of the students whose fathers are engaged in professional service are taking the classical course, while but 5 per cent of the children of common laborers are pursuing this course. For the commercial course, this range is from 62 per cent for transportation service to 9 per cent for professional service. The range is not so large for the other three curricula, but it is considerable and large enough to be significant. As a general thing, the scientific and general courses are patronized in greater proportion by the non-labor groups, while the reverse is true for the practical arts course.

Since the Mt. Vernon High School system consists of an academic and a vocational school, it is of interest to note the differences in the social composition of the students attending the two institutions. This is easily done by combining the data for the three academic curricula, on the one hand, and for the two vocational curricula on the other, as presented in Table XIX. The results of this process, followed by a reduction to percentages, are given in Table XX. A glance at this table makes it clear that these two high schools are appealing to different elements in the population. It seems that the children of laborers who do go to high school attend the vocational school almost altogether. To be sure, the non-labor groups also send a reasonable proportion of their children to this school but they exhibit a strong inclination to favor the academic school. They supply 84.6 per cent of the students in the latter and but 47.1 per cent of those in the former.

TABLE XIX

Number and Percentage of Students from Each Occupational Group Pursuing Each of the Five Curricula. Boys and Girls Combined.
Mt. Vernon High School

Parental Occupation	Number						Percentage					
	Classical	Scientific	General	Practical Arts	Commercial	Total	Classical	Scientific	General	Practical Arts	Commercial	Total
Proprietors	143	40	66	3	52	304	47	13	22	1	17	100
Professional service	74	18	22	3	11	128	58	14	17	2	9	100
Managerial service	78	26	45	4	28	181	43	14	25	2	16	100
Commercial service	47	16	39	2	18	122	39	13	32	2	14	100
Clerical service	20	9	15	2	21	67	30	13	23	3	31	100
Agricultural service	1	1	....	3	5	11	9	9	....	28	45	100
Artisan-proprietors	18	1	13	1	5	56	32	2	23	....	45	100
Building trades	8	5	3	1	19	57	14	9	23	2	34	100
Machine trades	3	4	3	10	32	57	14	7	5	18	56	100
Printing trades	1	1	3	4	14	25	12	4	12	16	56	100
Miscellaneous trades	1	1	1	....	1	4	25	25	12	16	25	100
Transportation service	9	1	4	2	16	32	28	3	13	6	50	100
Public service	4	2	4	....	16	26	15	8	15	....	62	100
Personal service	1	....	....	3	5	9	11	....	....	33	56	100
Miners, lumber-workers, fishermen	....	....	2	1	3	3	....	....	33	17	50	100
Common labor	....	....	....	....	1	1	....	....	....	....	100	100
Unknown	1	2	....	5	9	18	5	11	6	28	50	100
	11	5	9	1	11	37	30	13	24	3	30	100
Total	419	131	228	44	262	1,084	39	12	21	4	24	100

TABLE XX

Percentage of Students in Each of the Mt. Vernon High Schools Coming from Each Occupational Group

Parental Occupation	Academic High School	Vocational High School
Proprietors	32.0	18.0
Professional service	14.7	4.6
Managerial service	19.2	10.5
Commercial service	13.1	6.5
Clerical service	5.6	7.5
Artisan-proprietors	4.6	6.5
Agricultural service	.4	2.6
Building trades	1.9	13.8
Machine trades	.9	5.9
Printing trades	.4	.3
Miscellaneous trades	1.8	5.9
Transportation service	1.3	5.2
Public service	.1	2.6
Personal service	.3	1.3
Miners, lumber-workers, fishermen	.0	.3
Common labor	.5	4.6
Unknown	3.2	3.9
Total	100.0	100.0

In Figure 14 an attempt has been made to measure the relative attractiveness of the two schools to the several occupational divisions. It is based on the number of children in the vocational school for every one hundred from the same group in the academic school. In order to get numbers sufficiently large to insure reliability, several of the labor groups were combined, as indicated in the diagram. The difference between the two extremes is indeed striking. The proportion of children

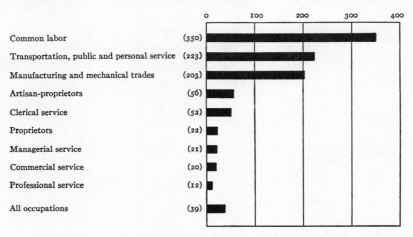

FIG. 14.—Showing for each occupational group the number of students (both sexes and all classes) in the vocational high school for every 100 from the same group in the academic high school. Data from 306 students in the former and 778 in the latter. Mt. Vernon.

from the professionals, the commercial workers, the managers, and the proprietors attending the vocational school is very small. The reverse is true for the children of the laboring classes, particularly laborers of the lower grades. The clerical workers and the artisan-proprietors occupy an intermediate position.

ST. LOUIS

The course of study in the St. Louis High Schools is more complex than that in any of the other cities studied. There are four-year, two-year, and one-year courses. Altogether, thirteen different curricula are offered, of which two are for girls exclusively, three for boys only, and eight for both boys and girls. The following descriptive statements adapted from the printed outlines distributed to the parents will give the reader some notion of the character of these curricula:

I. *Four-year courses.*—Seven four-year courses are offered with a basic requirement of one half-year community civics, one half-year of vocations, three or four years of English, and one or more years of history common to all.   These curricula with their distinctive features are:

1. *General course.*—One or more years of science and other subjects to be chosen from specified lists for each half-year.   In the third and fourth years of this course, there is a wide election offered, including units peculiar to other courses.

2. *Scientific course.*—Four years of mathematics; four years of science; two or three years of a foreign language.

3. *Classical course.*—Four years of Latin; two or three years of one other foreign language, if elected; one, two, or three years of mathematics, if elected; one or two years of science.

4. *Fine-arts course.*—Four years of art or music; one or more years of science; one or more years of mathematics, if elected; two or more years of a foreign language, if elected.

5. *Manual training course.*—Three or four years of manual training; three or four years of mechanical drawing; two, three, or four years of mathematics; one, two, or three years of science; two years of a foreign language, if elected.

6. *Home economics course.*—Four years of household arts; three or four years of science; one, two, or three years of mathematics, if elected; and two or three years of a foreign language, if elected.

7. *Commercial course.*—Four years of commercial branches grouped in sequence; one, two, or three years of mathematics, if elected; one, two, or three years of science; two or three years of a foreign language, if elected.

II. *Two- and one-year vocational courses.*—Four two-year and two one-year vocational courses are offered.   Very little academic material is included in these curricula.   They are as follows:

1. *Two-year manual training course.*—Joinery, turning, pattern-making, forging, tool-making, machine-shop practice, mechanical drawing, English, mathematics, and physics.

2. *Two-year home economics course.*—Household arts, English, botany, physiology, and chemistry.

3. *Two-year commercial course.*—Business English, commercial arithmetic, civics, commercial geography, penmanship, bookkeeping, stenography, typewriting, and spelling.

4. *Two-year vocational course in printing.*—Printing, shop practice, English, drawing, civics, vocations, industrial history, shop mathematics.

5. *One-year bookkeeping course.*—Business English, commercial arithmetic, penmanship, spelling, bookkeeping, and typewriting.

6. *One-year stenographic course.*—Business English, spelling, stenography, and typewriting.

The number of children from each of the occupational groups pursuing each of the curricula is given in Table XXI for the entire high-school population. Separate data for the boys and girls are presented. For convenience, since the number taking either course is small, the one-year bookkeeping course and the one-year stenographic course are combined under the "one-year commercial course." A glance at the totals shows practically all the girls enrolled in four curricula, namely, the general, four-year commercial, four-year home economics, and two-year commercial. Likewise, almost 90 per cent of the boys are found in the general, scientific, four-year commercial, and four-year manual training courses. It is interesting to note the status of the classical course with its 67 boys and girls, a mere vestige that tells very little of its glorious past. This curriculum has undoubtedly seen better days. Several of the short vocational courses have not, as yet at least, gripped the attention of children of high-school age. With the other curricula offered it is clear that St. Louis is offering its children an enriched high-school curriculum.

Let us see how the boys and girls representing the different social groups react to this diversity of curricular opportunity. A careful examination shows practically the same tendencies at work here as those discovered in Bridgeport and Mt. Vernon. The case is not quite so clear, perhaps, because the lines between the courses are not so plain. St. Louis has no curriculum that can be regarded strictly as college preparatory, unless it be the little-patronized classical course. Perhaps the general course and the scientific course come nearest to it. At least, they do not point out into industry.

Among the girls the home economics course is apparently about equally popular with all the occupational groups, although some slight tendency toward a greater proportional representation in this course on the part of the non-labor groups is observable. This constitutes some evidence favorable to the contentions of certain critics of the courses offered in this field that they do not prepare for wage-earning. The four-year commercial course attracts the daughters of the manual

TABLE XXI

SELECTION OF CURRICULA BY CHILDREN FROM THE VARIOUS OCCUPATIONAL GROUPS, ST. LOUIS HIGH SCHOOLS (WHITE), ALL CLASSES

Boys

Parental Occupation	General	Scientific	Commercial	Manual Training	Classical	Fine Arts	Two-Year Commercial	Two-Year Manual Training	Two-Year Printing	One-Year Commercial	Total
Proprietors	405	96	97	173	3	15	25	15			829
Professional service	197	37	7	60	8	3	8	3			323
Managerial service	248	48	50	147	3	10	23	20	1		550
Commercial service	194	33	46	88	3	5	4	12	1	1	397
Clerical service	92	24	35	60	3	6	9	4	1		234
Agricultural service	10	1	4	2			1	1			19
Artisan-proprietors	65	26	40	42	1	1	7	13	2		207
Building trades	51	21	26	52	1		19	25	2		197
Machine trades	50	12	15	80	1		16	24			199
Printing trades	16	3	10	15		2	4				50
Miscellaneous trades	43	17	42	45	2		16	14	2		181
Transportation service	54	8	32	44			14	16	1		169
Public service	17	1	5	13			3	4			45
Personal service	12	2	4	8			6	2			34
Miners, lumber-workers, fishermen								1		1	1
Common labor	6	6	6	4		1	5	4		1	26
Unknown	40		14	19			9	8		1	98
Total	**1,500**	**335**	**433**	**852**	**26**	**44**	**189**	**167**	**10**	**3**	**3,559**

Girls

Parental Occupation	General	Scientific	Commercial	Home Economics	Classical	Fine Arts	Two-Year Commercial	Two-Year Home Economics	One-Year Commercial	Total
Proprietors	384	6	150	96	7	40	87	2	2	774
Professional service	211	2	39	32	13	19	20	1	1	338
Managerial service	344	4	140	65	9	32	80	1	3	678
Commercial service	220	2	74	41	3	18	60		3	421
Clerical service	151		65	35	5	5	51	1	3	316
Agricultural service	24	1	7	2		2	8			44
Artisan-proprietors	55	2	48	26	2	8	49		3	191
Building trades	59	2	64	18	1	3	80	1	3	231
Machine trades	63	1	63	14		6	82		2	231
Printing trades	23		13	5		1	18			60
Miscellaneous trades	37	2	54	7		4	78	2	3	181
Transportation service	75		66	23		2	51	4	3	228
Public service	29		21	2		2	11		1	66
Personal service	12		14	3	1		16			47
Miners, lumber-workers, fishermen	1		1				2			4
Common labor	11		8	1			22	1		43
Unknown	55	1	34	7	1	3	19	1	2	123
Total	**1,754**	**23**	**861**	**377**	**41**	**145**	**734**	**14**	**29**	**3,978**

laborers more than the girls from other classes. But the most significant comparison is the one to be drawn between the general and the two-year commercial courses. In Table XXII this comparison is made. Here is given the percentage of the girls from each of the occupational groups found in these two curricula. On the one hand, professional service leads in the general course and takes last place in the two-year commercial course with 62.4 per cent and 5.9 per cent respectively of its

TABLE XXII

PERCENTAGE OF GIRLS FROM EACH OCCUPATIONAL GROUP PURSUING THE GENERAL AND THE TWO-YEAR COMMERCIAL COURSES, ST. LOUIS HIGH SCHOOLS, ALL CLASSES, DECEMBER, 1920

Parental Occupation	General Course	Two-Year Commercial Course
Professional service...................	62.4	5.9
Agricultural service...................	54.5	18.2
Commercial service...................	52.3	14.3
Managerial service....................	50.7	11.8
Proprietors...........................	49.6	11.2
Clerical service.......................	47.8	16.1
Public service........................	43.9	16.7
Printing trades.......................	38.3	30.0
Transportation service................	32.9	22.4
Artisan-proprietors...................	28.8	25.7
Machine trades.......................	27.0	35.2
Building trades.......................	25.5	34.6
Common labor........................	25.5	51.2
Personal service......................	25.5	34.0
Miners, lumber-workers, fishermen........	25.0	50.0
Miscellaneous trades..................	20.4	43.1
All occupations....................	44.1	18.5

representatives in the two courses. On the other hand, but 20.4 per cent of the girls whose fathers are engaged in the miscellaneous trades have chosen the first course; and 51.2 per cent of the daughters of common laborers are pursuing the second. The other groups fall in between these two extremes, with the non-labor groups inclining disproportionately toward the general course and the labor groups toward the two-year commercial course. Many other interesting observations will be made here by the careful reader.

As in Bridgeport, the boys appear to be less influenced in their choice of courses than the girls by the social groups from which they come. An examination of Table XXI shows the labor groups somewhat better represented in the commercial and manual training courses than the other groups, but only slightly so.   This may mean that the outlook from the four courses, in which most of the boys are enrolled, is, after all, very much the same.   The commercial course for the girls probably means preparation for a clerical position to be entered upon immediately after leaving school, whereas the same course taken by a boy may mean, particularly in the Middle West, college preparation.   Data secured in response to the question about expectations following graduation suggest this conclusion.   More evidence appears in Figure 15 in

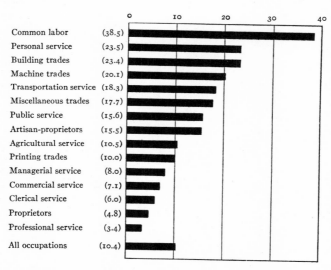

FIG. 15.—Showing the percentage of boys from each occupational group pursuing the two- and one-year vocational courses.   St. Louis high schools (white).

which is presented the percentage of the boys in each of the occupational classes registered in the one- and two-year vocational courses.   Obviously these curricula do not point collegeward.   Consequently, it is not surprising to see rather pronounced differences among the groups.   Here is the already familiar order with common labor at one extreme, and professional service at the other.

Before leaving the returns from St. Louis it will be worth while to examine with some care the social composition of the boys and girls to be found in two of the curricula registering but few students—the classical and fine arts courses.   The first is distinctly reminiscent of the time when secondary education was avowedly selective in its character; and the second is one of the newer courses which is supposed to rest on the possession of some special talent or is regarded as a preparation for a life of leisure. The occupations of the fathers of the students (boys and girls combined) pursuing these two curricula are given in percentages in Table XXIII. Apparently the prestige of the classical course carries but little weight with the laboring classes. Note, on the other hand, the extraordinarily disproportionate representation of the

TABLE XXIII

PERCENTAGE DISTRIBUTION OF THE OCCUPATIONS OF THE FATHERS OF 67 STUDENTS PURSUING THE CLASSICAL COURSE AND 189 THE FINE ARTS COURSE IN THE ST. LOUIS HIGH SCHOOLS, ALL CLASSES

Parental Occupation	Classical Course	Fine Arts Course
Proprietors.	15.0	29.1
Professional service	31.3	11.6
Managerial service	17.9	22.2
Commercial service	8.9	12.2
Clerical service	11.9	5.8
Agricultural service	. . . .	1.1
Artisan-proprietors	1.5	4.7
Building trades.	4.5	1.6
Machine trades.	3.0	3.7
Printing trades.	1.5	.5
Miscellaneous trades.	. . . .	1.1
Transportation service	. . . .	2.1
Public service	3.0	1.1
Personal service	. . . .	1.1
Miners, lumber-workers, fishermen	. . . .	. . . .
Common labor.	. . . .	. . . .
Unknown.	1.5	2.1
Total.	100.0	100.0

professionals. Almost one-third of these students come from this group which constitutes less than 9 per cent of the total high-school population. The fine arts course also is not a course for the children of labor, as is clearly seen. To what extent this is due to lack of talent is an unanswered question. But it is probable that the explanation is to be found in neither the presence nor the absence of talent, but in circumstance.

SEATTLE

In the high schools of Seattle there are seven curricula, of which six are open to the girls and six to the boys, although practically no boys are found in one of them. They are all four-year courses with the opportunity for electives ranging all the way from seven to eighteen credits[1] out of a total of thirty-two. In addition to a uniform requirement for all courses of six credits in English and two credits in United States History and Civics, the seven curricula may be described as follows:

I. *The academic course* emphasizes the traditional academic subjects and points toward the higher education, although each of the curricula offered may prepare for college, if the student exercises a little prudence in the choice of electives, because of the latitude in the entrance requirements among the colleges of the West.   This course includes five credits in mathematics, two in science, two in history besides the common requirement, four in one foreign language, and eleven electives.

II. *The general course* is designed for those students who are not definitely decided on their educational future.   Over one-half of the required number of credits are elective.   The prescribed subjects are two credits in algebra, two in history, two in laboratory science, and eighteen electives.

III. *The commercial course* prepares for clerical positions and includes seventeen credits in the ordinary commercial subjects, allowing but seven elective credits.

IV. *The industrial arts course* is really not so industrial as it sounds. But six credits in shopwork and mechanical drawing are required. The remainder of the course is composed of mathematics, history, laboratory science, and eleven elective credits.

V. *The home economics course* includes two credits in mathematics; two in chemistry; six in food, clothing, and design; two in household management; and twelve electives.

VI. *The art and crafts course* makes but a narrow appeal, although it does provide opportunity for the election of twelve credits.   It prescribes two credits in mathematics, two in laboratory science, and eight in art or craft.

VII. *The music course* likewise attracts but few students.   It is composed of two credits in mathematics, two in history, four in foreign languages, two in science, six in music, and eight electives.

The facts pertaining to the selection of curricula are presented in Table XXIV.   The academic course is seen to be the most popular among both girls and boys.   The number taking the art and crafts and fine arts courses is very small, almost negligible.   A comparison with Bridgeport and St. Louis shows the commercial course to attract a much larger proportion of the girls in the East than in the West.   Thus in

[1] A credit here means a semester's work in a particular subject.

Bridgeport 50.2 per cent of all the girls in the high school are enrolled in this course; while in St. Louis this percentage drops to 40.8; and in Seattle it drops still farther to 26.1. It is possible that this difference may be explained in terms of reduced expectations of college attendance on the part of girls in the East due to the practical absence of the great co-educational state universities common in the West.

TABLE XXIV

SELECTION OF CURRICULA BY CHILDREN FROM THE VARIOUS OCCUPATIONAL GROUPS IN THE SEATTLE HIGH SCHOOLS, ALL CLASSES

PARENTAL OCCUPATION	GIRLS							BOYS					
	Academic	General	Commercial	Home Economics	Art and Crafts	Music	Total	Academic	General	Commercial	Industrial Arts	Art and Crafts	Total
Proprietors.........	251	131	111	29	20	1	543	297	151	40	36	2	526
Professional service..	224	84	36	18	19	4	385	187	77	20	34	.....	318
Managerial service...	226	151	135	53	25	2	592	227	144	40	48	1	460
Commercial service..	140	77	44	23	10	1	295	128	64	23	23	1	239
Clerical service......	54	51	43	18	6	1	173	56	32	10	10	.....	108
Agricultural service..	53	36	43	18	7	.....	157	63	48	14	11	.....	136
Artisan-proprietors...	20	22	39	6	3	1	91	23	24	8	11	1	67
Building trades	83	114	102	34	19	3	415	89	112	46	59	3	300
Machine trades	60	68	94	26	10	3	261	67	65	12	44	3	191
Printing trades	14	15	6	1	1	.....	37	12	10	2	4	.....	28
Miscellaneous trades.	23	21	24	8	1	.....	77	19	17	6	2	.....	44
Transportation service	59	30	84	22	5	1	201	62	54	15	14	.....	145
Public service.......	8	15	27	6	1	1	58	11	13	8	3	.....	35
Personal service.....	13	25	16	10	.....	.....	64	10	10	8	7	.....	35
Miners, lumberworkers, fishermen.	8	17	14	4	.....	.....	43	3	6	4	4	.....	17
Common labor......	9	20	17	5	.....	.....	51	10	19	7	1	.....	37
Unknown...........	37	42	38	12	.....	.....	129	49	45	12	13	1	120
Total..........	1,282	919	933	293	127	18	3,572	1,313	891	275	324	12	2,815

As in the other cities studied, the girls from the different occupational groups in the Seattle high schools exhibit characteristic tendencies in the choice of curricula. This is brought out best in Table XXV, in which the probable distribution of one hundred girls from each of the groups over the six courses offered is given. The arrangment of the table is based on the proportion to be found in the academic course. There is seen to be a distinct negative correlation between choice of the academic and choice of the commercial course. For example, fifty-eight out of every hundred of the girls whose fathers are engaged in the professional pursuits are registered in the former course, while but nine are taking the latter. On the other hand, among the daughters of public servants, chiefly policemen and city firemen, but fourteen out of a hundred are to be found in the former and forty-six in the latter course. On the whole, the non-labor groups incline toward the academic and the labor groups toward the commercial course. The other courses appear to be almost equally attractive to both of these groups, although there is perhaps some slight observable disposition on the part of the girls whose

TABLE XXV

PROBABLE DISTRIBUTION OF 100 GIRLS FROM EACH OCCUPATIONAL GROUP OVER THE SIX COURSES OPEN TO GIRLS IN THE SEATTLE HIGH SCHOOLS, ALL CLASSES

Parental Occupation	Academic Course	General Course	Commercial Course	Home Economics Course	Art and Crafts Course	Music Course	Total
Professional service	58	22	9	5	5	1	100
Commercial service.	48	26	15	8	3	. . . .	100
Proprietors.	46	24	21	5	4	. . . .	100
Managerial service.	38	26	23	9	4	. . . .	100
Printing trades	37	41	17	3	2	. . . .	100
Agricultural service.	34	23	27	12	4	. . . .	100
Clerical service.	31	30	25	11	3	. . . .	100
Miscellaneous trades	30	27	31	11	1	. . . .	100
Transportation service. . .	29	15	42	11	3	. . . .	100
Machine trades.	23	26	36	10	4	1	100
Artisan-proprietors.	22	24	43	7	3	1	100
Personal service.	20	39	25	16	. . . . . .	. . . .	100
Buildings trades.	20	27	39	8	5	1	100
Miners, lumber-workers, fishermen	19	40	33	8	. . . . . .	. . . .	100
Common labor.	18	39	33	10	. . . . . .	. . . .	100
Public service	14	26	46	10	2	2	100
All occupations.	36	26	26	8	4	. . . .	100

fathers are engaged in manual labor to choose the general course in disproportionate numbers. This, in all probability, is due to greater uncertainty about the future on the part of these students. It is interesting to note here, as in St. Louis, the failure of the home economics course to make any large appeal to the daughters of laborers. It seems that, for various reasons, these girls are interested primarily in courses that relate rather definitely to wage-earning.

Table XXVI, showing the probable distribution of one hundred boys from each occupational group over the five curricula open to boys, is arranged on the same principle as the table immediately previous giving similar facts for the girls. The two curricula to be contrasted here are

the academic and general courses.   The first draws especially from the
non-labor groups, with professional service leading, while the students
choosing the second come in larger proportion from the labor groups.
The contrast is not so pronounced as among the girls, but it is sufficiently
marked to be significant.   It is surprising, perhaps, that there are no

TABLE XXVI

PROBABLE DISTRIBUTION OF 100 BOYS FROM EACH OCCUPATIONAL GROUP OVER THE
FIVE CURRICULA OPEN TO BOYS IN THE SEATTLE HIGH SCHOOLS,
ALL CLASSES

Parental Occupation	Academic Course	General Course	Industrial Arts Course	Com- mercial Course	Art and Crafts Course	Total
Professional service........	59	24	11	6	....	100
Proprietors..............	57	29	7	7	....	100
Commercial service......	53	27	10	10	....	100
Clerical service..........	52	30	9	9	....	100
Managerial service.......	49	31	11	9	....	100
Agricultural service.......	47	35	8	10	....	100
Miscellaneous trades......	43	39	4	14	....	100
Printing trades...........	43	36	14	7	....	100
Transportation service....	43	37	10	10	....	100
Machine trades...........	35	34	23	6	2	100
Artisan-proprietors.......	34	36	16	12	2	100
Public service............	31	37	9	23	....	100
Building trades............	29	36	19	15	1	100
Personal service..........	29	29	20	22	....	100
Common labor...........	27	51	3	19	....	100
Miners, lumber-workers, fishermen..............	17	35	24	24	....	100
All occupations......	47	32	11	10	....	100

clear tendencies shown in the choice of the two vocational curricula—
the industrial arts and commerical courses.   It is true that certain of the
labor groups are much better represented in these curricula than any of
the non-labor groups.   On the other hand, some of the labor groups
have very poor representation.   It should be borne in mind, however,
that none of these Seattle curricula points exclusively toward industry
or commerce and away from college.

CONCLUSION

Certain conclusions stand out very clearly in the light of this analysis
of practice in the several cities studied.   The children coming into the
public high school from the different occupational groups exhibit differ-

ent tendencies in their election of curricula. Those occupations that have relatively poor representation in the high school patronize the "practical" courses, the courses which point outward toward wage-earning rather than upward toward higher education. The lower the grade of occupation, the stronger this tendency manifests itself. The girls are apparently influenced in larger measure than the boys by the occupational status of the parent.

CHAPTER IX

PARENTAL OCCUPATION AND EXPECTATIONS FOLLOWING GRADUATION

Closely related to a student's choice of curricula are his expectations following graduation, since presumably the various curricula are organized around different objectives. This relation, however, is not always sustained in individual cases. Many instances can be found of students pursuing the college preparatory curricula who do not expect to attend college. And one would not have to seek far to find children enrolled in the commercial course who are not planning to enter into clerical work. Consequently it will be of interest to make a study of the relation between parental occupation and expectations following graduation from high school as a supplement to the material presented in the immediately previous chapter.

In each of the four cities studied this question was asked of each student: "What do you intend to do following graduation from high school?" There were, of course, a few students in each high school who reported that they did not intend to complete the course. In tabulating the data their intentions on leaving the high school were accepted in lieu of the usual statement of expectations following graduation.

But of what value are the responses to this question? May they be regarded as possessing any measure of truth? Certainly, as indices of what these students are actually going to do after graduation, they are far from satisfactory. In considering their future prospects, these young people in all probability err on the side of optimism, as most people would. Many of those who, in their Freshman year, speak with some confidence of their intentions to attend college or university after graduation from high school will never complete the high-school course, let alone grace the halls of an institution of higher learning. On the other hand, there will probably be some whose plans to attend college will crystallize only toward the end of their stay in the secondary school. It is not maintained, therefore, that these responses have a great deal of objective validity; but it is believed that group-differences, to the degree they are revealed here, have significance. It seems likely that the optimistic bias would be exhibited equally by the various groups, or at least that the bias, in so far as it exists in varying measure among

74

the groups, would tend to minimize rather than exaggerate the differences that actually exist.

Since the expectations of the two sexes following graduation are somewhat different, the presentation divides itself into two parts, the one dealing with the girls, and the other with the boys. The order of treatment will be as just indicated.

EXPECTATIONS OF THE GIRLS

For purposes of tabulation, the various activities into which the girls expect to go are classified under twelve headings, namely, college or university, normal school, business college, other school, professional service, clerical service, commercial service, industrial service, home, travel, work, and undecided. The meaning of each of these is clear with the possible exception of the eleventh, *work*. In some cases the response was the very general statement that the student intended to go to work after leaving the high school. The kind of work was not specified. Cases of this type are included under this category.

The gross data for the four cities are given in Table XXVII. According to this table, the largest group, 36.5 per cent of the entire number, are intending to go to college. Over 13 per cent are going to normal school, business college, or other higher schools. Of those who do not plan to continue their education, by far the largest number, practically one-fourth of the total, are going into the clerical occupations. About 5 per cent will engage in professional service, chiefly nursing and teaching. Very few are looking toward either the commercial or industrial occupations. Practically none are looking forward to travel. Perhaps the most interesting fact in the table is the number expecting to remain at home. Only 82 of the 9,286 girls reporting have their eyes on the domestic life, according to their own statements. Of course these returns should not be taken too seriously, since at this particular point the question about expectations is a rather personal one. Although there were a few girls who state very frankly that they expect to "get married," the ordinary high-school girl has a natural reluctance about exhibiting too much certainty about a very uncertain matter. Nevertheless, it is apparent that the great majority of the girls of this generation are looking forward to an active life in the world of affairs after leaving the high school. Apparently they are not so domestic as were their mothers and grandmothers. In addition to these statements of specific expectations, a small group merely report that they are going to work, and 14.4 per cent are undecided. In conclusion, the general observation may be made that in these high schools the attention of the girl students is rather strongly directed toward a continued education, and especially toward the college.

TABLE XXVII

EXPECTATIONS FOLLOWING GRADUATION OF 9,286 GIRLS IN THE HIGH SCHOOLS OF BRIDGEPORT, MT. VERNON, ST. LOUIS, AND SEATTLE

Expectations Following Graduation	Bridge-port	Mt. Vernon	St. Louis	Seattle	Total	Per-centage
College..	241	186	1,340	1,624	3,391	36.5
Normal school	294	4	146	81	525	5.7
Business college	16	49	166	247	478	5.1
Other school	25	34	63	101	223	2.4
Professional service	39	25	197	217	478	5.1
Commercial service	. . . .	6	10	. . . .	16	.2
Clerical service	443	136	1,208	522	2,309	24.9
Industrial service	2	. . . .	21	12	35	.4
Home.	1	4	64	13	82	.9
Travel.	. . . .	. . . .	3	5	8	.1
Work.	27	2	171	201	401	4.3
Undecided.	132	70	589	549	1,340	14.4
Total.	1,220	516	3,978	3,572	9,286	100.0

If the returns from the various cities are examined and compared, some interesting differences are noted.   Bridgeport and Seattle represent the two extremes.   In the former but 19.4 per cent of the girls are intending to go to college as compared with 45.5 per cent in the latter. The other side of this comparison is found in the proportion expecting to enter the clerical occupations.   In Bridgeport this proportion mounts to 36.3 per cent, while in Seattle it falls to but 14.6 per cent.   These differences are probably to be explained in terms of population and geography.   As contrasted with Seattle, the population of Bridgeport is predominantly industrial and largely of the new immigration.   Also the tradition of a higher education for women is not so strong in the East as in the West.   The presence of a great state university, the University of Washington, is another important factor in explaining the strong college tendency among the girls of the Seattle high schools.

The table also shows considerable variation in the proportion of students looking toward the normal school.   In Bridgeport 24 per cent of the girls are planning to attend teacher-training institutions.   In Mt. Vernon, on the other hand, this proportion falls to .8 per cent; and in Seattle and St. Louis it is but 2.3 and 3.7 per cents respectively.

This large number in Bridgeport intending to enter the normal school probably explains in some measure the small proportion planning to enter college. The presence of a city normal school in Bridgeport is an important factor in accounting for this situation, although the Harris Teachers' College of St. Louis does not seem to have a similar effect there. Another matter worthy of comment in this connection is the small number of students outside of Bridgeport thinking about entering teacher-training institutions. Clearly these cities are not producing their own future teachers.

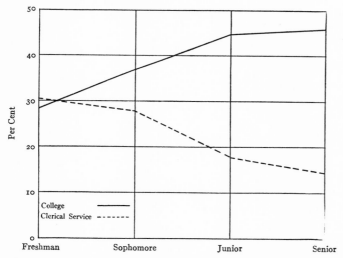

FIG. 16.—Showing the percentage of girl students in each of the high-school years intending either to go to college or to enter clerical service following graduation. Data from 9,286 girls in the high schools of Bridgeport, Mt. Vernon, St. Louis, and Seattle.

The characteristic differences in the intentions exhibited by the students in the four years of the high school are shown graphically in Figure 16 in which the percentage of girls in each year expecting to go to college is compared with the corresponding percentage for those planning to enter the clerical occupations. The proportion looking toward the college begins at 28.5 per cent in the Freshman year and rises to 45.8 per cent in the Senior year. The clerical service shows just the reverse tendency. In the first year of the high school there are actually more girls expecting to engage in clerical work on leaving high school than there are preparing for college, 30.4 as against 28.5 per cent, to be exact.

This proportion, however, falls rapidly, as the other rises, and in the last year of the high school it is reduced to 14.3 per cent. This is an excellent exhibition of the strength of the college-preparatory tradition in the public high school. It is to be explained in terms of both elimination and adaptation.

We come now to the more important part of the study—that pertaining to the parental occupation. A detailed table showing the complete distribution of the girls from each occupational group will not be given,

TABLE XXVIII

PERCENTAGE OF GIRLS FROM EACH OCCUPATIONAL GROUP INTENDING TO GO TO COLLEGE, ENTER NORMAL SCHOOL, OR ENGAGE IN CLERICAL WORK ON LEAVING HIGH SCHOOL. DATA FROM 9,286 STUDENTS IN BRIDGEPORT, MT. VERNON, ST. LOUIS, AND SEATTLE

Parental Occupation	College	Normal School	Clerical Service
Proprietors	49.4	4.5	12.0
Professional service	61.8	4.0	7.7
Managerial service	41.1	6.1	19.9
Commercial service	47.1	3.4	17.3
Clerical service	33.3	6.0	27.4
Agricultural service	33.6	7.1	21.8
Artisan-proprietors	23.9	6.1	36.9
Building trades	17.3	5.4	35.7
Machine trades	19.0	8.9	40.3
Printing trades	33.0	....	26.0
Miscellaneous trades	13.5	8.7	45.9
Transportation service	23.1	6.2	30.8
Public service	21.3	9.8	32.3
Personal service	18.6	6.4	37.1
Miners, lumber-workers, fishermen	25.5	....	29.8
Common labor	14.6	4.3	50.0
All occupations	36.5	5.7	24.9

since it would contribute nothing of consequence that cannot be presented in a more simplified form. The percentage of students intending to pursue each of the three more important lines of activity is presented for each set of occupations in Table XXVIII. It shows that 49.4 per cent of the girls whose fathers or guardians are occupied as proprietors are expecting to attend college, 4.5 per cent to go to normal school, and 12.0 per cent to enter the clerical service following graduation from high school. The remaining 34.1 per cent, not included in this table, are distributed over the other nine activities. Tremendous differences among the occupational groups are observed. The percentage intending to go to college ranges all the way from 61.8 for professional service to 13.5 for the miscellaneous trades. In the main, the labor groups are low and the non-labor groups high in the frequency of college expectations. The reverse is true with respect to the proportion planning to enter the clerical occupations. Note the range from 7.7 per cent for professional service to 50.0 per cent for common labor. The normal school apparently is attracting the attention of students from the various occupations impartially. In no single group do we find any marked tendency toward teacher-training institutions.

Special attention is directed in Table XXIX to the composition of that group of girls in the high school who are intending to go to college.

TABLE XXIX

PERCENTAGE DISTRIBUTION OF THE OCCUPATIONS OF THE FATHERS OR GUARDIANS OF 3,391 GIRLS IN ALL FOUR HIGH-SCHOOL YEARS AND OF 688 GIRLS IN THE SENIOR YEAR WHO ARE INTENDING TO GO TO COLLEGE. BRIDGEPORT, MT. VERNON, ST. LOUIS, AND SEATTLE

Parental Occupation	All Four Years	Senior Year
Proprietors	24.6	24.4
Professional service	15.6	17.7
Managerial service	19.0	20.3
Commercial service	11.8	12.2
Clerical service	5.7	5.4
Agricultural service	2.4	2.1
Artisan-proprietors	2.7	2.6
Building trades	3.7	3.3
Machine trades	3.8	2.9
Printing trades	1.0	.6
Miscellaneous trades	1.4	1.2
Transportation service	3.3	2.6
Public service	1.0	.3
Personal service	.8	1.0
Miners, lumber-workers, fishermen	.3	.3
Common labor	.5	.3
Unknown	2.4	2.8
Total	100.0	100.0

One-half of the table gives in percentages the occupations of the fathers or guardians of the entire number of girls in all four years of the high school who are looking toward college; the other gives similar data for this particular group in the Senior year. It will be seen at once that these girls come from a very restricted section of the population. Five occupational groups (proprietors, professional service, managerial service, commercial service, and clerical service) include 76.7 per cent of all the girls expecting to enter college. In an earlier chapter it was observed that these five groups accounted for but 71.5 per cent of all the students in the Senior year.   Thus the group of girls going to college, enrolled in all four years, shows a considerably higher degree of selection than the complete registration of the Senior year.   Relatively speaking, the daughters of the laboring classes do not look forward to the higher education.

Furthermore, the second half of this table makes it clear that this selection continues to operate from year to year with the result that exactly 80 per cent of the girls in the last year of the high school who

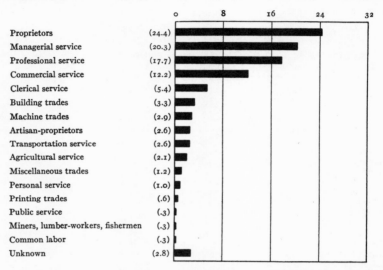

FIG. 17.—Showing by percentages the occupations of the fathers or guardians of 688 girls in the Senior year of the high school who are intending to go to college. Bridgeport, Mt. Vernon, St. Louis, and Seattle.

are planning to go to college come from the five groups just named. These facts are presented graphically in Figure 17.   If the artisan-proprietors and agricultural service be set aside as not strictly labor groups, the contribution of the laboring classes is reduced to but 12.5 per cent, and it seems altogether probable in the light of evidence already presented that this representation of labor will be further reduced when the roll is called in the Freshman year of college.   These statements on the part of high-school Seniors are in some cases certainly no more than expressions of desire which will have to give way before the facts of life.

One other relation should be examined before passing to an analysis of the expectations of the high-school boys.   It is the relation between the occupational groups in the different years of the high school. And for purposes of economy a comparison will be made between but two of the groups, the professional service and the machine trades. The former represents the tendency among the non-labor, while the latter is typical of the labor groups. The comparison is drawn in Figure 18. In the Freshman year the widest differences are noted. Here 58.5 per cent of the girls from professional homes are intending to go to college. All the forces of home and tradition are pointing them in that direction. It is a question that is settled for them. They do not have to think

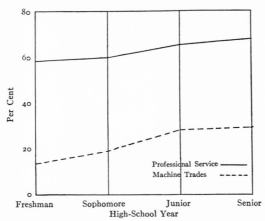

FIG. 18.—Showing for each of two occupational groups the percentage of girls in each year of the high school intending to go to college. Bridgeport, Mt. Vernon, St. Louis, and Seattle.

about it. On the other hand, of the girls in this first year whose fathers are engaged in the machine trades, only 13.7 per cent are looking toward the college. As we pass up through the years, we see the proportion going to college increasing for each group, until in the Senior year, the percentage is 67.8 for the one, and 29.0 for the other. The increase for the machine trades is the larger. This is, in all probability, to be explained through the strong college-preparatory tradition which the student encounters in the high school, as well as through greater elimination among those no intending to go on to college.

EXPECTATIONS OF THE BOYS

Naturally the classification of activities for the boys, though fundamentally the same as that used for the girls, has its characteristic features. "Normal school" and "home" are eliminated, and in addition to the remaining categories of the previous classification, "agriculture," "transportation service," and "public service" are included. Under these thirteen headings it was found possible to group the expectations of all the boys.

TABLE XXX

EXPECTATIONS FOLLOWING GRADUATION OF 7,979 BOYS IN THE HIGH SCHOOLS OF BRIDGEPORT, MT. VERNON, ST. LOUIS, AND SEATTLE

Expectations Following Graduation	Bridgeport	Mt. Vernon	St. Louis	Seattle	Total	Per-centage
College.................	655	340	1,822	1,796	4,613	57.8
Business college..........	9	6	17	27	59	.8
Other school.............	40	15	80	59	194	2.4
Professional service.......	11	7	37	24	79	1.0
Commercial service.......	32	27	114	89	262	3.3
Clerical service..........	33	46	196	44	319	4.0
Industrial service.........	33	29	92	101	255	3.2
Transportation service	....	....	11	5	16	.2
Public service............	2	....	3	8	13	.2
Agriculture..............	1	....	13	12	26	.3
Travel...................	....	....	2	7	9	.1
Work....................	47	27	598	168	840	10.5
Undecided...............	174	71	574	475	1,294	16.2
Total..............	1,037	568	3,559	2,815	7,979	100.0

Table XXX shows the college tradition to be much stronger among the boys in these four cities than among the girls. Of all the boys in high school, 57.8 per cent are intending to go to college, according to their own statements. No other line of activity is attracting a sufficiently large number to be worthy of comment. Slightly over 16 per cent are "undecided" and 10.5 per cent are just going to "work," but these categories are so general as to make it unnecessary to qualify the preceding statement.

An examination of the facts for the different cities shows no such variation here as was found for the girls. In each city over one-half of the boys are looking toward the college. If Bridgeport and Seattle are compared, it is discovered that the percentages of such boys in the high schools of the two cities are almost identical, being 63.2 and 63.8 respectively. It will be remembered that the corresponding percentages for the girls were 19.4 and 45.5. These figures are illustrative of a tendency noted at several points in this study, namely, that the girls appear to represent the social class from which they come more than do the boys. The industrial and immigrant character of the Bridgeport population provides little stimulus toward a college education.   The boys break over, the girls conform.

These differences between the boys and the girls are brought out more clearly in Figure 19.   From the first year to the last over 20 per cent more boys than girls are expecting to enter college.   This does not, of course, mean that all these boys will eventually go to college, but it does indicate that they regard college preparation as a very good explanation of their registration in the high school.   So far as the boys are concerned, it seems that the public high school is predominantly

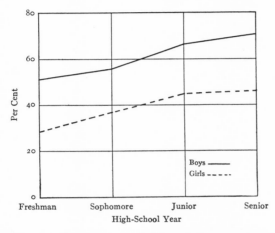

FIG. 19.—Showing the percentage of girls and the percentage of boys in each year of the high school intending to go to college.   Bridgeport, Mt. Vernon, St. Louis, and Seattle.

a college-preparatory institution in spirit, in spite of all the concessions made to the practical needs of those whose education must end with the high school.   This is not so true of the girls, because there is one curriculum in the high school which is very popular among them and which does point quite definitely to something besides the college—and that is the commercial course.   Nothing comparable to it for the boys is to be found in the ordinary high school.

Passing to a consideration of the relation between parental occupation and expectations following graduation, we shall merely call attention to the proportion from each group expecting to go to college.   An examination of the detailed distribution is of little significance.   These facts are given in Table XXXI.   A minute exposition of this table is unnecessary, since the results are much the same as those already discussed for the girls. This difference alone should be noted, that the boys from the laboring classes exhibit a relatively stronger college tendency than do the girls. There is slight tendency for them to follow in the footsteps of their fathers. Most of them look on the high school as a means of lifting themselves out of the class into which they were born.

TABLE XXXI

NUMBER AND PERCENTAGE OF BOYS FROM EACH OCCUPATIONAL GROUP INTENDING TO GO TO COLLEGE AFTER GRADUATION FROM HIGH SCHOOL IN BRIDGE-PORT, MT. VERNON, ST. LOUIS, AND SEATTLE, ALL CLASSES

Parental Occupation	Number	Percentage
Proprietors	1,152	66.4
Professional service	599	77.3
Managerial service	815	63.9
Commercial service	507	64.6
Clerical service	229	55.4
Agricultural service	106	59.6
Artisan-proprietors	163	47.1
Building trades	241	40.8
Machine trades	264	47.6
Printing trades	35	40.7
Miscellaneous trades	116	38.8
Transportation service	168	46.0
Public service	38	35.8
Personal service	39	39.8
Miners, lumber-workers, fishermen	3	15.8
Common labor	25	25.8
Unknown	113	44.3
Total	4,613	57.8

That there are, after all, important differences among the groups is shown in Figure 20, which presents for the boys the same comparison made for the girls in Figure 18. The percentages from both the professional service and the machine trades, in each year of the high school intending to go to college, are given. Large differences exist, but not so large as for the girls.

STUDENTS NOT EXPECTING TO COMPLETE THE HIGH-SCHOOL COURSE

As intimated at the beginning of this chapter, a few students were found who did not expect to complete the high-school course. It will be of interest to see from what elements in the population they come. Since the number in the three upper years is practically negligible, we shall confine our attention to the Freshman year.

Of the 6,782 students in the first year of the high schools in the four cities, only 451 expressed any doubt about their prospects of completing the course. Undoubtedly, many others were uncertain about the matter but failed to give expression to this uncertainty. The social composition of this group of children is given in Table XXXII. The first part of the table presents the actual distribution of the 451 students over the several

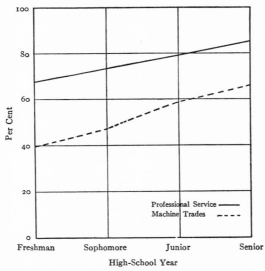

FIG. 20.—Showing for each of two occupational groups the percentage of boys in each year of the high school intending to go to college. Bridgeport, Mt. Vernon. St. Louis, and Seattle.

occupational groups; the second, the percentage of the children from each of the groups who do not expect to complete the course. For purposes of comparison, this latter part of the table is the more significant. In the main, it shows the order already familiar to the reader. The children whose fathers are engaged in the professional occupations exhibit the least uncertainty about their stay in the high school. Only 3.3 per cent of them do not expect to complete the course. The children of common laborers, on the other hand, show the greatest uncertainty. Exactly 20 per cent, or one in every five, are doubtful about remaining until graduation. The other groups fall in between these two extremes, with the laboring classes occupying the less favorable positions. Because of the small number of cases involved in some of the groups, too much weight should not be attached to their records. The unfavorable showing of the printing trades, for example, is probably to be explained in this way. Likewise, the relatively favorable position of personal

TABLE XXXII

Occupations of the Fathers or Guardians of 451 Students in the First Year of the High School Who Do Not Expect to Complete the Course, and the Percentage from Each Occupational Group Not Expecting to Complete the Course. Data from 6,782 Freshmen in the High Schools of Bridgeport, Mt. Vernon, St. Louis, and Seattle

Parental Occupation	Number	Percentage
Proprietors	43	3.6
Professional service	17	3.3
Managerial service	48	4.6
Commercial service	22	3.8
Clerical service	24	6.0
Agricultural service	17	10.5
Artisan-proprietors	14	4.7
Building trades	78	13.0
Machine trades	35	6.2
Printing trades	9	13.0
Miscellaneous trades	26	8.0
Transportation service	38	9.0
Public service	13	11.1
Personal service	6	6.3
Miners, lumber-workers, fishermen	5	16.1
Common labor	24	20.0
Unknown	32	13.3
All occupations	451	6.6

service would probably not be maintained in the face of more adequate data. On the whole, the evidence here supports the conclusions derived from the study of expectations following graduation.

CHAPTER X

THE PUBLIC HIGH SCHOOL AND THE CULTURAL LEVEL

All that has been said in the previous chapters about parental occupations has a very direct bearing on the relation of the public high school to the various social and cultural levels within a community. All the evidence presented indicates that the high school is, in the main, serving the occupational groups representative of the upper social strata. This seems to be true even in those cities where the proportion of children of high-school age attending the public secondary school is relatively large. Of course, the writer is quite conscious of the fact that social lines do not follow rigidly the occupational divisions, but he is firmly convinced that, within limits, the occupation is an immensely important, if not a decisive, factor in determining social status. One does not canvass the ranks of manual labor while seeking out the select "Four Hundred" of urban society. To be sure, individuals occasionally break the bonds of an occupation without leaving it, but such cases are rare. Also, family connections and inheritance may set aside or shift the incidence of the decrees of occupation, as manifested in economic power, social prestige, and cultural advantages. These, however, are not the rule. Thus far, the study shows the high school drawing its population from the higher cultural levels.

It is the purpose of this chapter to display an additional bit of evidence pointing in the same direction. In Bridgeport and Mt. Vernon, each high-school student was asked if there was a telephone in his home or the home in which he lived. This same question was asked the children in the compulsory continuation classes and the trade school in Bridgeport, as well as the pupils of the Mt. Vernon sixth grade. Returns on this item were not received from the students attending the Bridgeport Evening High School.

Obviously, the possession of a telephone is not an adequate index of cultural level. The resulting dichotomous classification of people makes of modern society an entirely too simple affair. It divides people into two hard and fast divisions—those who have telephones and those who have not. Clearly this is an over-simplification. It reminds us of the much-advertised classification of all men into two classes—the exploited and the exploiters. As useful as this may be for political purposes, and as true as it may be as a description of certain aspects of modern society, it does not give a truthful picture of people who, as a rule, are neither black nor white, but, on examination, are found to represent varying shades of gray.

Also, the possession of a telephone is not an infallible index of cultural level; some occupations demand a telephone in the home, others may require that it be absent. Undoubtedly, many persons do not have telephones in their homes who are living on a relatively high cultural plane and it is certain that the reverse is equally true. Yet, it must be admitted that the telephone is one of the many elements going to make up the cultured home. The correlation is not perfect, but it is positive.

An ideal investigation would have included returns on many other items, such as the number and character of books, magazines, and newspapers in the home, various other material possessions indicating comfort and taste, the character of the conversation, the interest in music and art, and a host of other things that are already in the reader's mind. But obviously, this ideal was not attainable in a study bounded by the ordinary limitations of investigation. A thorough investigation along lines here suggested of the cultural level and the standard of living of the homes from which high-school students come should make a valuable contribution toward the understanding of the problems which public secondary education is facing in this country.

The significance of the telephone, at least, as an index of general social and educational advancement, is shown in an impressive fashion in Figure 21. The data for this diagram are taken from the 1917 report of the Federal Census on Telephones, and *An Index Number for State School Systems*, by Ayres. The states, including the District of Columbia, were first arranged in order of their achievements in secondary education as measured by the percentage of the total school attendance credited to the high school in 1918. They were then grouped into five groups of ten states each, except the last, in which there are but nine. And finally, the number of telephones per thousand inhabitants was averaged for each of these groups of states. This figure forms the basis for the construction of the bars in the diagram.

It is clear that some relation between high-school attendance and the ratio of telephones to the population does exist. For the ten states ranking highest in the proportion of children attending high school, the average number of telephones per thousand inhabitants is 145, while the corresponding figure for the nine states ranking lowest in this respect is but 41. The relation, however, is not pronounced among the states at the upper end of this distribution. The first ten exceed the record of the second ten by two points only; and there is much overlapping between these two groups if the facts for individual states are examined. For the remainder of the distribution, on the other hand, there is relatively little overlapping, and the difference from group to group is marked. Of course, no claim is advanced that there is any large and direct causal relation between the number of telephones in a

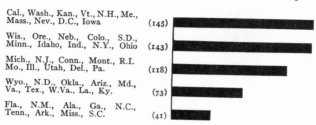

Cal., Wash., Kan., Vt., N.H., Me., Mass., Nev., D.C., Iowa	(145)
Wis., Ore., Neb., Colo., S.D., Minn., Idaho, Ind., N.Y., Ohio	(143)
Mich., N.J., Conn., Mont., R.I. Mo., Ill., Utah, Del., Pa.	(118)
Wyo., N.D., Okla., Ariz., Md., Va., Tex., W.Va., La., Ky.	(73)
Fla., N.M., Ala., Ga., N.C., Tenn., Ark., Miss., S.C.	(41)

FIG. 21.—Showing the average number of telephones per 1,000 inhabitants in five groups of states in 1917,[1] arranged in order of the percentage that high-school attendance was of total public-school attendance in 1918.[2]

[1] *Bureau of the Census, Census of Electrical Industries*, 1917, "Telephones," p. 22.
[2] L. P. Ayres, *An Index Number for State School Systems*, p. 37.

community and the attendance at high school. The one is certainly not the cause of the other. The installation of a telephone in a particular home will not, in some mysterious way, start the children of high-school age off to high school the following morning, if they have not been attending. It is much more likely that the two phenomena are both the effects of a common cause.

BRIDGEPORT

In the city of Bridgeport there are 115 telephones for every thousand inhabitants. This is only a moderate record, since the number ranges in American cities from about 50 to 250. A more serviceable figure for the purposes of this study is the number of telephones in residences alone. On March 31, 1921, there were 8,302 such telephones. Assuming that the average family in Bridgeport consists of approximately five persons, there were probably about 30,000 families in the city at the time the data for this study were collected. In other words, telephones are to be found in about 28 per cent of the homes.

The percentage of children in the high school, the trade school, and the compulsory continuation classes, in whose homes there are telephones, is graphically presented in Figure 22.   The children in the high school exhibit one extreme and those in the continuation classes the other; and the difference is indeed large.   Among the former, telephones are in almost 50 per cent of the homes, while in the latter

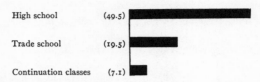

FIG. 22.—Showing the percentage of children in the high school, the trade school, and the compulsory continuation classes in whose homes there are telephones.   Data from 2,531, from 198, and from 421 cases respectively.   Bridgeport, February and March, 1921.

this percentage drops to approximately 7.   The former is far above, and the latter far below the percentage for the entire city, as given above.   The students in the trade school constitute an intermediate group, although here the percentage with telephones is somewhat smaller than for the population as a whole.   Clearly the high-school population is a socially favored group as measured by this single criterion of culture.

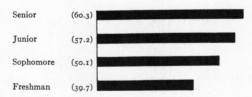

FIG. 23.—Showing the percentage of students in each year of the Bridgeport High School in whose homes there are telephones.   March, 1921.

A study of the four high-school years reveals the continued operation of this selective tendency.   An inspection of Figure 23 shows this to be true.   Here is given the percentage of students in each of the years or grades in whose homes there are telephones.   This advances from 39.7 per cent in the Freshman to 60.3 in the Senior year—an impressive advance.   A word of caution, however, should be thrown out here in making an interpretation of the facts as presented.   It seems probable that there are two influences working toward the same end.   On the one hand, there is the selective factor.   A disproportionately large number of those eliminated from high school come from homes in which there never have been and never will be telephones. On the other hand, the thought is worthy of consideration that continuation in high school may be a factor working for the installation of a telephone in the home. The social tone of the school and the associations formed probably cause these adolescents to bring pressure to bear on the parents favoring an expenditure for this purpose. There are many reasons why boys and girls of high-school age, particularly, should want telephones in their homes. Of course this factor operates outside, as well as

FIG. 24.—Showing the percentage of girls in each of three curricula in the Bridgeport High School in whose homes there are telephones. Data from 271, 376, and 715 cases respectively. March, 1921.

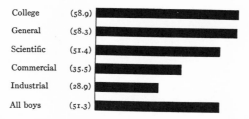

FIG. 25.—Showing the percentage of boys in each of five curricula in the Bridgeport High School in whose homes there are telephones. Data from 397, 562, 24, 141, and 45 cases respectively. March, 1921.

inside, the high school, but the social life of the school conceivably accentuates it. At any rate, the difference from year to year is significant.

In view of the findings already discussed, bearing on the relation of parental occupation to choice of curricula, there is a natural expectation that the percentage of students coming from homes with telephones varies with the courses. And this is exactly the case, as shown in Figure 24 and Figure 25. In the former are presented the facts for the girls, and in the latter for the boys. The girls in the college course appear to be the most highly selected group. Almost three-fourths of these students have telephones in their homes. The boys in the same course show no such measure of selection, although for them, the percentage having telephones is larger than in any other group of boys. The difference found here between the two sexes confirms the conclusions drawn in an earlier chapter that class lines are more closely drawn among the girls than among the boys. At the other extreme, as might be expected, is the commercial course for the girls and the industrial arts course for the boys, with 37.5 per cent and 28.9 per cent respectively of the students pursuing the two courses having telephones in their homes. The boys in the commercial course have about the same record as the girls. The general course is somewhat above the average, the scientific course only slightly so. Likewise, the normal course seems to attract a constituency that is just about on a level with the high-school population as a whole with respect to this single item of information. All these facts constitute corroborative evidence of the socially selective character of the various curricula offered in the Bridgeport High School.

MT. VERNON

It has already been pointed out that the population of Mt. Vernon, since it is a suburb of New York City, is somewhat selective. In large measure, it is a middle-class residential community. Consequently, the ratio of telephones to the population is considerably higher than in Bridgeport and somewhat higher than in most American cities.

Since data from the sixth grade are available, the contribution of Mt. Vernon to this part of the study has peculiar interest. While it is admitted that the pupils of the sixth grade are the product of a certain measure of selection, they do give a fairly reliable cross-section of the population of the city. Figure 26 is based on the percentage of children in each grade, for which data are available, in whose homes there are telephones. This percentage in the sixth grade is 44, and rises to 87.5 in the last year of the high school. Although operating at a higher level, due to certain general differences between the two cities noted in the previous paragraph, the same tendencies appear here as in Bridgeport. From the sixth to the twelfth grade there is a constant increase in the proportion of children coming from homes having telephones. The curve rises somewhat more rapidly between the Freshman and Sophomore years of the high schools than in any other interval. Whether this is a chance feature of the curve that might disappear with data from a larger number of cases, or to be explained in terms of especially rapid elimination between the first and second high-school years, it is impossible to speak with assurance. Conceivably it might be accounted for through the operation of some other factor, such as the influence of high-school attendance on the installation of a telephone in the home.   As a matter

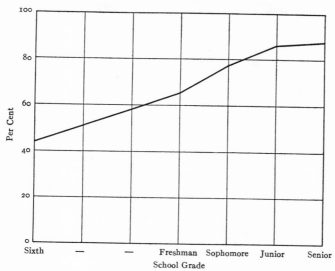

FIG. 26.—Showing for each grade from the sixth to the Senior year of the high school the percentage of children in whose homes there are telephones.   No data for the seventh and eighth grades.   Mt. Vernon, May, 1921.

of fact, an examination of the enrolments in the different grades does indicate that the elimination between the Freshman and Sophomore years is somewhat more pronounced than in the grades from the sixth

TABLE XXXIII

PERCENTAGE OF STUDENTS PURSUING EACH CURRICULUM IN WHOSE HOMES THERE ARE TELEPHONES, MT. VERNON HIGH SCHOOLS, ALL YEARS

Curriculum	Girls	Boys	Total
Classical....................	92.2	86.9	89.5
General.....................	77.6	82.5	79.8
Scientific...................	61.5	79.7	77.8
Commercial.................	57.3	52.7	55.7
Practical arts...............	....	34.9	34.1
All curricula................	76.2	75.2	75.5

to the ninth.   Whatever the explanation, the student in the Senior year of the Mt. Vernon high schools in whose home there is no telephone has a very small representation.

As in Bridgeport, there are interesting differences among the students choosing the various curricula. This is brought out clearly in Table XXXIII. The classical course, throughout the four high-school years, draws almost exclusively from students coming from homes where there are telephones. This tendency is somewhat more marked among the girls than among the boys. It seems that the girls from the well-to-do classes cling to the conventional course which carries with it the greatest social prestige. Note, in this connection, that in each case the two newer academic curricula (general and scientific) attract a somewhat smaller proportion of girls than boys from homes possessing telephones. The practical arts courses represent the other extreme, with the commercial course occupying an intermediate position. Telephones are found in the homes of only about one-third of the students pursuing the former curriculum. The fact that no girls in this course are from such homes should not be regarded seriously, since their number is very small.

CHAPTER XI

THE PUBLIC HIGH SCHOOL AND FAMILY INFLUENCES

In the American social order, large responsibilities respecting the care and education of the children are placed on the family. The measure of these responsibilities varies from place to place and it is not so great as in former times. The establishment of the public school and the passage of compulsory education laws have lightened the parental obligations and set limits to the parental authority in the domain of education. But, beyond the reach of these compulsory laws the family still holds its sway, and as a rule, the field of secondary education is in this realm. Consequently, it will be of interest to note the relation between certain family influences and the high-school population.

To a degree, all the sociological factors discussed in this monograph either determine or reflect home conditions. This is certainly true of parental occupation which is the backbone of the study. In this chapter, attention will be directed to certain of the narrower aspects of family life, including the mortality of parents, the occupation of the mother, the number of children, and the order of birth. This is not a particularly formidable array of family influences, nor is it at all complete. A much more detailed study is needed. Nevertheless, the study of these few factors will be seen to be significant and suggestive.

MORTALITY OF PARENTS

Perhaps there is no single incident in the life of the family that is more calamitous and disorganizing than the death of one of the parents before the children have reached maturity. This means that the natural balance between organ and function in the family is destroyed, and a readjustment involving, particularly, the status of the children is necessary before stability may again be secured. Of course, among the more fortunate economic classes, a storm of this sort may be weathered without undue sacrifice on the part of individual members, but these do not form a majority of the population. Again, some might maintain that divorce or separation is as serious a disintegrating factor as death itself, and much could be said in support of this view. But, except in cases of desertion, such occurrences are the fruitage of a longer

or shorter process of growth, during which adjustments of various
sorts may be contemplated and plans set in motion for their realization.
However, regardless of the conclusion on this particular point, it is clear
that the death of one of the parents is a serious matter.

Returns on this question were received from all the groups studied.
The percentage of students in the high schools of the four cities having
one or both parents deceased is given by sex and by city in Table XXXIV.
According to this table, 12.9 per cent of the entire number of 17,265
students have one or both parents deceased. The mortality seems to be
much higher among the fathers than among the mothers. This is
distinctly true in each of the cities studied, and the data for the different
high-school years show the same result. This is due to the greater age
of the fathers and to the higher rate of mortality among men. Both
parents are deceased in slightly over 1 per cent of the cases.

An examination of the facts from the different cities shows some
variation. The percentage is lowest in Bridgeport and highest in
Seattle, ranging from 12.3 in the former to 13.4 in the latter. The
explanation apparently is to be found in the proportion of children of
high-school age attending high school. The city maintaining a relatively
large high-school enrolment is, other things being equal, likely to have
in its high schools a larger proportion of children handicapped in various
ways than the city with the smaller proportionate enrolment. Evidence
bearing on this point will be presented in other parts of the chapter.

TABLE XXXIV

PERCENTAGE OF STUDENTS IN THE HIGH SCHOOLS OF BRIDGEPORT, MT. VERNON,
ST. LOUIS, AND SEATTLE HAVING ONE OR BOTH PARENTS DECEASED.
DATA FROM 17,265 CASES

PARENTAL MORTALITY	BRIDGEPORT			MT. VERNON			ST. LOUIS			SEATTLE			TOTAL		
	Girls	Boys	Both Sexes	Girls	Boys	Both Sexes	Girls	Boys	Both Sexes	Girls	Boys	Both Sexes	Girls	Boys	Both Sexes
Father deceased	7.6	4.9	6.4	7.4	8.8	8.1	7.8	7.5	7.6	8.1	7.0	7.8	7.8	7.3	7.5
Mother deceased	5.3	4.4	4.9	4.2	3.4	3.8	3.8	3.7	3.8	4.9	4.5	4.7	4.5	4.0	4.3
Both parents deceased	1.2	.8	1.0	1.2	1.2	1.2	1.6	.9	1.3	.8	.9	.9	1.2	.9	1.1
One or both deceased	14.1	10.1	12.3	12.8	13.4	13.1	13.2	12.1	12.7	13.8	12.9	13.4	13.5	12.2	12.9

The table also shows important differences between the sexes. The
percentage of girls having one or both parents deceased is somewhat
larger than the percentage of boys. This is true in each of the cities
except Mt. Vernon, and is to be explained in the same way as the differ-

ences among the cities.   In every city, except Mt. Vernon, the number of
boys in high school is appreciably less than the number of girls.   The
boys are consequently a more highly selected group with the result that
fewer of them are handicapped by the loss of a parent.   Putting it in
another way, from the standpoint of securing a secondary education,
the death of a parent is a more serious matter to the boy than to the
girl.   Apparently the burden of earning the family livelihood is more
likely to fall on the one than on the other.

A fundamental question should be raised here.   Does the 12.9 per
cent of children in high school who have lost one or both parents indicate
that loss of a parent diminishes the educational opportunities of the
child?   What proportion of the children of high-school age have lost
one or both parents by death?   This is a rather difficult question to
answer, although an answer may be approximated by using certain
data furnished by the Federal Census.   We know the average age of the
high-school student and we know the average age of the parents of
the student.   Then assuming that the father was alive a year before the
child was born, and taking from the United States Life Tables the
mortality rates for the ages desired, it is an easy task to estimate the
mortality of the parents of children of high-school age.   The average
age of high-school students is about sixteen years and the average ages
of the fathers and mothers are approximately forty-eight and forty-three
years respectively.   Since all the fathers were alive seventeen years and
all the mothers sixteen years before this census of high-school students
was taken, it remains merely to compute the mortality rate for the seven-
teen- and sixteen-year periods respectively, beginning at thirty-one years
for the fathers and twenty-seven for the mothers.   In this way, after
making certain slight additional computations, it is found that at least
24 per cent of children of high-school age have lost one or both parents
by death.   This is to be compared with the 12.9 per cent for high-school
students.   After making due allowance for the occasional student who
reports a step-father or step-mother as an actual parent, and for the very
rough method of calculation just used, the difference between these two
percentages is altogether striking.   There is apparently a strong relation
between life or death of the parent and the educational opportunity of
the child.

There is much corroborative evidence secured in this investigation
that supports the conclusions of the previous paragraph derived from
estimates and calculations.   The change from year to year in the percentage of high-school students who have lost one or both parents is

shown in Table XXXV. An examination of this table makes it clear that this percentage changes very little in passing from the Freshman to the Senior year. The difference of .4 per cent between these two years is too small to be of any significance whatsoever. Undoubtedly, during the three calendar years that separate the students in these two high-school grades, the parents of these students are not living under a condition of immunity from death. There is no good reason for believing that this unwelcome visitor passes over the homes of high-school students. Assuming then that the life tables apply to the parents of these children as to other folk, and assuming further that there is no selective elimination of those losing parents, the percentage of high-school students having one or both parents deceased should rise more than five points from the Freshman to the Senior year, or from 12.7 to at least 17.7.

TABLE XXXV

PERCENTAGE OF STUDENTS IN EACH YEAR OF THE HIGH SCHOOL HAVING ONE OR
BOTH PARENTS DECEASED. DATA FROM 17,265 CASES IN BRIDGEPORT,
MT. VERNON, ST. LOUIS, SEATTLE

High-School Year	Bridgeport	Mt. Vernon	St. Louis	Seattle	Total
Freshman....	10.7	14.8	12.4	13.4	12.7
Sophomore...	14.3	10.9	13.0	12.8	12.9
Junior.......	13.8	12.4	12.6	13.9	13.2
Senior.......	10.8	14.0	13.1	13.9	13.1
Total....	12.3	13.1	12.7	13.4	12.9

In Mt. Vernon, returns on this question of mortality of parents were secured from all children in the sixth grade. Again assuming no selective elimination, the percentage of children who have lost one or both parents should be considerably higher in the high school than in the sixth grade. But such is not the case. The percentage is actually more than two points lower in the former than in the latter, being 13.1 and 15.3 respectively. Reasoning from the life tables, the figure for the sixth grade approximates the expectation, although it is from 1 to 2 per cent lower. Instead of being lower for the Senior year of the high school than for the sixth grade, it should be seven or eight points higher. The evidence here, therefore, reflects very clearly the importance of the life of the parent in promoting school attendance.

The data from the various groups of children of high-school age are illuminating in this connection. In Figure 27 the group of 514 children of high-school age in Seattle is compared with the high-school population of the same city. Although the former are on the average slightly younger than the latter, 21.7 per cent of the children at work have lost one or both parents as against but 13.4 per cent of the high-school students.

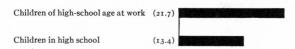

Children of high-school age at work (21.7)

Children in high school (13.4)

FIG. 27.—Showing percentage of children in each of two groups having one or both parents deceased. Data from 514 children of high-school age at work and 6,387 children in high school. Seattle, 1919–20.

The four groups from Bridgeport present an even more striking comparison. Examine Figure 28 in which the facts for the evening high school, the compulsory continuation classes, the state trade school, and the day high school are presented graphically. In interpreting this diagram it should be kept in mind that the students in the trade school are of about the same age as those in the regular high school, while those in the evening high school average a year and one-half older, and

Evening high school (31.7)

Continuation classes (21.6)

State trade school (18.2)

Day high school (12.3)

FIG. 28.—Showing percentage of children in each of four groups having one or both parents deceased. Bridgeport, 1920–21.

the children in the continuation classes are a half-year younger. With these considerations in mind, the comparisons made in this diagram take on significance. Practically one out of every three students in the evening high school has lost a parent. The mortality among the parents of this group is more than two and one-half times the mortality among the parents of high-school students. It should be greater by 3 or 4 per cent because of the age differences, but no more than that. Thinking in terms of ages, the percentage should be higher for the high school than for the continuation classes, but the reverse is true in actual fact, to the extent of more than 9 per cent. Because of its two-year course and its practical bent, the trade school enrols a larger proportion of children who have been unfortunate in this respect than does the high school.

One other bit of evidence bearing on this question is presented in Table XXXVI. In the previous chapter it was pointed out that between 6 and 7 per cent of the students in the Freshman class do not expect to complete the course, according to their own statements. In three of the cities, Bridgeport, Mt. Vernon, and St. Louis, the relation of this matter to mortality of parents was worked out for the first-year students, and the results are given in this table. It will be noted that there is a much larger percentage who have lost their parents among

TABLE XXXVI

PERCENTAGE OF STUDENTS IN EACH OF TWO GROUPS HAVING ONE OR BOTH PARENTS DECEASED. DATA FROM 4,437 STUDENTS IN THE FRESHMAN YEAR OF THE HIGH SCHOOL IN BRIDGEPORT, MT. VERNON, AND ST. LOUIS

Group	Girls	Boys	Both Sexes
Students in the Freshman class not expecting to complete the high-school course..	20.6	22.1	21.4
All students in the Freshman class........	12.8	11.9	12.4

those who do not expect to complete the course than among the students of the entire Freshman class. To be exact, the percentages are 21.4 and 12.4 respectively. Furthermore, this tendency is decidedly more marked for the boys than for the girls. Thus, while in the general high-school population the girls show a higher proportion having deceased parents than the boys, in that part of the student body not expecting graduation the reverse is true. Both facts support the conclusion that disorganization of the family falls more heavily on the boy than on the girl.

OCCUPATION OF THE MOTHER

It is well known that in many American families the mother engages in remunerative labor outside the home and in this way contributes to the family support. It is clear that, from the standpoint of the home, this is a disintegrating influence, or, at least, is evidence of disintegration. In most cases the mother is forced to carry this extra burden because of economic pressure, and it therefore may be ordinarily regarded as an indication of poverty. It is apparent, however, that this is not true in all cases, for occasional reports in this study indicate that rare instances of the "emancipated" woman do appear. Some women with families are demanding and are getting the privilege of earning their own livings in their own ways.

Data were secured from the students in the high schools of all four cities showing the extent to which their mothers were contributing to the support of the family. Similar data were also obtained from all the non-high-school groups except the children of high-school age at work in Seattle. Two questions were asked each individual, the one checking the other. The returns are relatively complete and are thought to be accurate.

Of the 17,265 high-school students included in the study, 1,289 or 7.5 per cent reported their mothers to be engaged in remunerative employment of some kind outside the ordinary duties of the housewife. There is some variation from city to city. The highest percentage of 10.3 is found in Seattle. Then follows Bridgeport with 6.9, St. Louis with 5.6, and finally, Mt. Vernon with 5.4. These differences are to be

Sixth grade   (15.6)

High school   (5.4)

Fig. 29.—Showing the percentage of children in the sixth grade and in the high school whose mothers are engaged in remunerative employment. Mt. Vernon, May, 1921.

explained in terms of the high-school enrolment and the occupational character of the population. For example, the large enrolment in the Seattle High School accounts for the high percentage of working mothers, since the deeper strata of the population are reached by the schools. Mt. Vernon, on the other hand, also has a relatively large proportion of its children in high school, but a low percentage of working mothers. This is probably due to the exceptional strength of the middle classes in this city.

The facts for the successive high-school years show a constant decrease in the proportion of working mothers from the first year to the last. Thus, the percentage decreases from 8.9 in the Freshman, to 7.5 in the Sophomore, 6.1 in the Junior, and 5.3 in the Senior year. This change, to be sure, is not startling but it is large enough to be significant.

An examination of the returns for Mt. Vernon is of special interest, because of the inclusion of the sixth grade in the study. In Figure 29 a comparison of the high school and the sixth grade shows marked differences between the two groups. The latter has almost three times

as large a proportion of working mothers as the former.   If this situation
is representative of American cities, we may say that, while it is uncom-
mon for the mothers of high-school students to contribute to the family
support by engaging in remunerative work, this condition obtains quite
frequently among the children of the elementary school.

As a final contribution to this topic, a comparison of the four Bridgeport groups is presented in Figure 30.   Again observe the clear differences

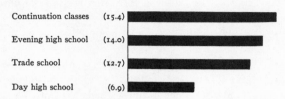

Continuation classes	(15.4)
Evening high school	(14.0)
Trade school	(12.7)
Day high school	(6.9)

FIG. 30.—Showing percentage of children in each of four groups whose mothers
are working at remunerative employment.   Bridgeport, 1919–20.

in the social character of the young people brought together in
these various schools and classes.   At the one extreme are the compulsory continuation classes in which 15.4 per cent of the mothers are working outside the home, and at the other, according to expectations, the
high school with a corresponding percentage of but 6.9.

BROTHERS AND SISTERS

It is natural to suppose that the number of children in the family
is an important factor in determining the richness of the opportunity
to be offered a particular child.   Some have advocated limiting the
birth-rate on the grounds that fewer children mean greater advantages
for those who are born.   And the decreasing birth-rate in wide sections
of the population is one of the most fundamental tendencies in western
society today.

In our investigation, inquiry was made as to the number of brothers
ànd sisters of each child in all the groups studied, except the students
in one of the Seattle high schools and the children at work in the same
city.   The general data for the high-school students are presented in
Table XXXVII.   A glance at the total number of students having
each indicated number of brothers and sisters shows a distribution
definitely skewed toward the lower end.   The most frequent number
of brothers and sisters is one, and a large proportion of these children
have none at all.   The medians also indicate that high-school students

come from rather small families. By adding one to the median, we get the number of children in the family. This would make three the median number of children in the families of the students in the high schools of these four cities. There is some variation among the cities, which is probably explained in terms of the racial character of the population. Thus, the larger families in Bridgeport and Mt. Vernon are certainly due to the influence of the newer immigrant stocks, among which the birth-rate is still high.

TABLE XXXVII

NUMBER OF HIGH-SCHOOL STUDENTS IN FOUR CITIES HAVING EACH INDICATED
NUMBER OF BROTHERS AND SISTERS

Number of Brothers and Sisters	Bridgeport	Mt. Vernon	St. Louis	Seattle	Total
0............	270	119	1,294	696	2,379
1............	485	287	1,952	1,212	3,936
2............	465	232	1,565	1,036	3,298
3............	376	177	1,082	690	2,325
4............	241	102	712	490	1,545
5............	186	60	408	290	944
6............	114	55	252	169	590
7............	59	18	139	97	313
8............	30	14	71	65	180
9............	16	16	41	23	96
10............	9	4	18	12	43
11............	1	....	2	4	7
12............	5	....	1	2	8
13............	....	....	....	....	....
14............	....	....	....	1	1
Total....	2,257	1,084	7,537	4,787	15,665
Median..	2.3	2.1	1.8	2.0	2.0

We see no evidence of the elimination of the students coming from the larger families as we pass from the Freshman to the Senior year. An examination of the facts shows that the median number of brothers and sisters for the students in the first year is exactly the same as it is for those in the last, namely, two. Even the very large families are as well represented in the later as in the earlier years. Furthermore, the proportion of "only" children remains constant from year to year. It would seem, therefore, that, among those elements in the population which do get their children into the high school, the size of the family is not an important factor in further influencing attendance.

A comparison, however, of the high-school population with the pupils in the sixth grade in Mt. Vernon does reveal some substantial differences. As already stated in Table XXXVII, the median number of brothers and sisters for the former is 2.1. The corresponding figure for the children of the sixth grade is 3.0. But this difference is not to be construed as meaning that children are kept out of high school because of membership in large families, for the matter is not quite so simple as that. A more reasonable interpretation is that the size of the family is being limited by those classes in the population from which most of the high-school students come.

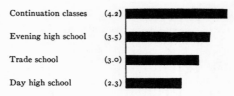

Continuation classes   (4.2)

Evening high school   (3.5)

Trade school   (3.0)

Day high school   (2.3)

FIG. 31.—Showing median number of brothers and sisters for the children in each of four groups. Bridgeport, 1920–21.

Data from the three groups of children in Bridgeport of high-school age not in high school give similar results. The medians for these groups and the students attending the high school in the same city are presented graphically in Figure 31. The difference between the continuation classes and the high school is really striking, but the interpretation suggested in the previous paragraph in all probability holds here. It is becoming clearer and clearer, however, that there are certain social strata that are not reached by the public high school.

ORDER OF BIRTH

Is the order of birth a matter of consequence to the child? In a society in which no law of primogeniture operates, is it best to be born first or last? On the basis of the returns to the two questions—(1) How many brothers and sisters have you? and (2) How many are older than you?—an effort was made to throw some light on the matter. It was found very difficult, however, to disentangle the various factors involved, particularly in the study of the high-school groups alone, because the proportion of firstborn children in the high schools of a particular community is in some measure a function of population movements. In a new and rapidly developing community, inhabited by the younger generation, the proportion of firstborn in the high school will be disproportionately large, because of the youthful character of the adult population. Many of their firstborn and relatively few of their lastborn children will be in high school. We shall therefore merely refer to the data from Bridgeport where the high-school population may be compared with other groups of children of high-school age.

The results of the study in Bridgeport are given in Table XXXVIII. For purposes of comparison, the relation between the firstborn and the lastborn is expressed in a single figure, namely, the number of the latter

TABLE XXXVIII

NUMBER OF FIRSTBORN FOR EVERY 100 LASTBORN CHILDREN
IN EACH OF FOUR GROUPS OF CHILDREN OF
HIGH-SCHOOL AGE IN BRIDGEPORT

High school	117
Trade school	121
Evening high school	159
Continuation classes	178

for every one hundred of the former in each of the four groups. The striking thing about the table, perhaps, is the relatively large proportion of firstborn to lastborn children. In any total population they ought to be equal, since only those families are included in which there are two or more children. In each of such families there is always a firstborn and a lastborn child, even in the case of twins. What then is the explanation of the total situation in Bridgeport? It is that suggested in the previous paragraph. Bridgeport has grown very rapidly during recent years; its population is therefore relatively youthful; and consequently, the proportion of firstborn among children of high-school age is considerably greater than that of lastborn children. The latter have not yet reached this age in proportionate numbers. But the table shows wide differences among these groups. The high school has the smallest proportion of firstborn children and the continuation classes have the largest. The inference is clear that the firstborn children are handicapped in the struggle of life. On them, more than on their younger brothers and sisters, falls the burden of contributing to the family support.

CHAPTER XII

THE PUBLIC HIGH SCHOOL AND THE IMMIGRANT

For at least three-quarters of a century we, as a nation, have faced the problems arising from the presence of a large immigrant population. Driven largely by economic considerations on the one hand and political forces on the other, the Irish and the Germans arrived in great numbers in the decade from 1845 to 1855. Since that time, up to the year of the Great War, with fluctuations due to the operation of various sociological forces, our immigration increased in volume and complexity. Gradually, as the years passed, the proportion from the less accessible and more backward countries of southern and eastern Europe increased, until toward the close of the nineteenth century we began to speak of the "new" immigration in contradistinction to the "old" from the north and west of Europe, which was culturally and racially more nearly allied to our own people. Today we are peculiarly conscious of the difficulties that attend the union of such diverse population elements.

In recent years much has been said and written about the relation of the immigrant to the public school, and numerous investigations have been made. Consequently this chapter will be cut down to its narrowest limits, and is included at all chiefly in the interests of a more complete sociological picture. Yet there are certain novel features of this study that will perhaps appeal to the reader.

Data bearing on this question were obtained in but two of the cities, Bridgeport and Mt. Vernon. Because of the small number of children of immigrant parentage in the schools of the latter, major attention will be given to the former. Although information concerning the country of birth for each parent was secured, the classification of the children in every instance follows the nativity of the father. This simplifies the tabulation of the data without detracting from the validity of the interpretation.

THE TOTAL ENROLMENT

As pointed out in an earlier chapter, the city of Bridgeport has a very large and varied immigrant population. In Table XXXIX the 2,257 students in the Bridgeport High School are classified according to the father's country of birth. For the sake of simplicity but ten divisions are used in this classification. In each case national units and boundaries are recognized as they existed in 1914, except that Poland is given distinct treatment. All the people from the old Austro-Hungarian Empire are grouped together, partly because the data did not in all cases indicate the particular part of this polyglot empire from which the fathers came. Under the British Empire are included all sections of the empire peopled by the white races, except Ireland. This has the merit at least of being satisfactory to most Irishmen and many

TABLE XXXIX

NATIVITY OF THE FATHERS OF 2,257 STUDENTS IN THE BRIDGE-
PORT HIGH SCHOOL

Country of Father's Birth	Number	Percentage
United States....................	1,106	49.0
Austria-Hungary.................	207	9.2
British Empire (excluding Ireland)..	155	6.9
Germany........................	51	2.3
Ireland.........................	174	7.7
Italy...........................	109	4.9
Poland.........................	25	1.1
Russia..........................	294	13.0
Scandinavia.....................	108	4.7
All others	28	1.2
Total......................	2,257	100.0
Total foreign	1,151	51.0

Englishmen, as well as being justified sociologically. Norway, Sweden, and Denmark, following the customary practice, are classed together as Scandinavia. An effort was made to keep the Hebrews separate, but without success. They are consequently assigned to the particular countries in which they were born; but, from the information given concerning the language spoken in the home, it is evident that practically all fathers born in Russia are really Russian Jews.

According to this table the fathers of 49 per cent of the students in the Bridgeport High School were born in the United States. The remaining 51 per cent are of immigrant parentage, and are widely distributed over the countries of Europe, with Russia leading and Austria-Hungary occupying second place. But these figures have no special significance when taken by themselves. Let us, therefore, pass to some comparative data.

THE FRESHMAN AND SENIOR YEARS

A comparison of the Freshman and Senior years is of interest. In Figure 32 is shown, for each of the groups, the number of students in the Senior year for every one hundred in the Freshman year of the high school. At the top stands Germany with 61.1, while Poland foots the list with but 15.4. The United States occupies an intermediate

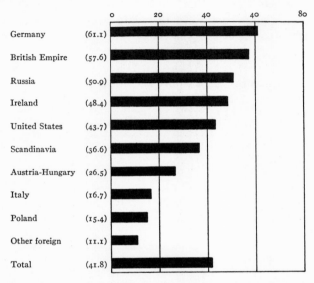

Fig. 32.—Showing for each ethnic group the number of students in the Senior year for every 100 in the Freshman year of the high school. Data from 2,257 cases. Bridgeport.

position. On the whole the people from the north and west of Europe make a better showing than those from the south and east. The single exception to this generalization is the case of Russia, whose large Hebrew contingent is probably responsible for the fact that the people from this section of Europe are found in third place. These conclusions are supported by the data from Mt. Vernon.

CHILDREN OF HIGH-SCHOOL AGE NOT IN HIGH SCHOOL

More significant perhaps than this comparison between the Freshman and Senior years is the comparison of the children in high school with the three groups outside, already studied in other connections. These are the children in the evening high school, the trade school, and the compulsory continuation classes. The facts are presented in Table XL in percentages. It is observed at once that children of native parentage are less well represented here than in the high school, while the reverse is true for the children of immigrants, taking them altogether. But an examination of the different immigrant stocks reveals great variation among them. A comparison of the percentages for these three groups with those for the high school given in the previous table shows greater proportional representation in the high school for the Irish, Russian Jews, and Scandinavians. In fact the Irish and the Russian Jews make almost as good a record as the native stock with their advantageous

TABLE XL

Nativity of the Fathers of Children in Evening High School, Trade School, and Compulsory Continuation Classes, Bridgeport

Group of Children	United States	Austria-Hungary	British Empire	Germany	Ireland	Italy	Poland	Russia	Scandinavia	All Others	Total Percentage	Number of Cases
Evening high school..	22.6	21.4	7.0	5.8	9.9	9.5	4.1	13.6	4.1	2.0	100.0	243
Trade school	22.2	26.3	8.6	5.0	2.0	13.2	5.6	6.0	6.6	4.5	100.0	198
Continuation classes	17.8	33.7	7.5	3.2	1.8	24.2	5.9	3.7	1.7	.5	100.0	579
Total	19.8	29.3	7.6	4.2	3.8	18.5	5.4	6.5	3.2	1.7	100.0	1,020

social and economic position. At the other extreme are the peoples of Austria-Hungary, the Italians, and the Poles, among whom the proportional representation is much greater in the three groups of children not in high school than in the high-school population. Another interesting feature of the table is the much greater representation of the Irish and the Russian Jews in the evening high school than in the trade school and the continuation classes. This indicates an unusually strong interest in an academic education on the part of these races, as well as exceptional energy and earnestness in the pursuit ôf educational opportunity, since voluntary attendance at evening school at best involves serious immediate, personal sacrifice.

The percentage of children in each of these four Bridgeport groups whose fathers were born in the United States is shown in Figure 33. Clearly the opportunities of secondary education are much more widely distributed among children of native parentage than among those born of immigrants.

A single set of facts from Mt. Vernon should be presented here. Owing to the very small numbers of children from most of the immigrant stocks in the schools of this city, it is hardly worth while to make the detailed analysis that has just been made for Bridgeport. There is one immigrant group, however, that is very well represented—the Italians. Consequently in Table XLI is given the number of children in the sixth grade and each year of the high school from each of three

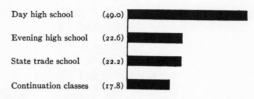

Day high school   (49.0)

Evening high school (22.6)

State trade school   (22.2)

Continuation classes (17.8)

Fig. 33.—Showing the percentage of children in each of four groups whose fathers were born in the United States. Bridgeport.

groups—the native stock, the Italians, and all others. Again, it is to be observed that the children of native parentage make a superior record and that among the other races the children of Italian fathers have an almost negligible representation in the later high-school years. For every one hundred children in the sixth grade the native stock has 30.2 in the last year of the high school; the Italians but 3.5; and all other immigrant groups 20.2.

TABLE XLI

NATIVITY OF FATHERS OF CHILDREN IN THE MT. VERNON SIXTH GRADE AND IN EACH YEAR OF THE MT. VERNON HIGH SCHOOLS

Country of Father's Birth	Sixth Grade	Freshman	Sophomore	Junior	Senior	Total
United States......	295	234	194	133	89	945
Italy.............	256	59	29	8	9	361
All others	188	132	99	60	38	517
Total........	739	425	322	201	136	1,823

THE CHOICE OF CURRICULA

It is interesting to see how the different racial groups respond to the curricular opportunities offered in the Bridgeport High School. Since the curricula for the girls are somewhat different from those for the boys, the two sexes will receive separate consideration.

In Table XLII are presented the curricular choices of the girls, grouped according to the nativity of the father. For convenience in comparison the distribution of each group of girls is expressed in percentages. Thus, of the 634 girls whose fathers were born in the United States, 24 per cent are pursuing the college preparatory course, 27 per cent the normal course, etc. If we note the percentage of girls from each of the groups pursuing each of the three popular curricula, some rather pronounced differences will be observed. The tendency for girls of native parentage to enter the college preparatory course is

TABLE XLII

PERCENTAGE OF GIRLS IN EACH GROUP PURSUING EACH OF THE CURRICULA OPEN
TO GIRLS IN THE BRIDGEPORT HIGH SCHOOL. GIRLS GROUPED
ACCORDING TO NATIVITY OF FATHERS

Curriculum	United States	Austria-Hungary	British Empire	Germany	Ireland	Italy	Poland	Russia	Scandinavia	All Others	Total	All Foreign
College..................	24	18	22	14	7	5	17	23	9	27	21	16
Normal..................	27	23	36	25	40	28	25	21	24	20	27	28
Commercial.............	47	54	42	57	52	67	50	55	62	53	50	54
General.................	2	3	.....	4	1	.....	8	1	5	.....	2	2
Scientific...............	.....	2	.....	.....	.....	.....	.....	.....	.....	.....	.....	.....
Total...............	100	100	100	100	100	100	100	100	100	100	100	100
Number of cases......	634	97	88	28	100	43	12	145	58	15	1,220	586

apparently considerably stronger than among girls of foreign parentage. Yet among certain of the immigrant groups, especially the Russian Jews and the people of the British Empire, excluding Ireland, the proportion to be found in this curriculum is almost as large as it is for the native stock. The Italians and the Irish are representative of the other extreme. The latter incline rather strongly toward the normal course. In fact 40 per cent of the Irish girls are planning to teach. The Russian Jews, on the other hand, show the least inclination in this direction. It is a fact worthy of attention in this connection that this curriculum is attracting a slightly larger percentage of the immigrant than of the native stock. The commercial course is also somewhat more attractive to the former, probably because of their lower social and economic level. Two-thirds of the Italian girls are enrolled in this course. Yet in Bridgeport, in every one of these groups, the percentage in the commercial course is larger than that to be found in any one of the other curricula.

It would be natural to suppose that the boys from these different groups behave somewhat as the girls do, but such is not the case, as a glance at Table XLIII shows. In contrasting the boys of native parentage with those of immigrant stock, it will suffice to confine our attention to but two of the curricula, the college preparatory and the scientific. No significant differences appear in the choice of the other curricula. Throwing all the immigrant groups together it will be

TABLE XLIII

PERCENTAGE OF BOYS IN EACH GROUP PURSUING EACH OF THE CURRICULA OPEN
TO BOYS IN THE BRIDGEPORT HIGH SCHOOL. BOYS GROUPED
ACCORDING TO NATIVITY OF FATHERS

Curriculum	United States	Austria-Hungary	British Empire	Germany	Ireland	Italy	Poland	Russia	Scandinavia	All Others	Total	All Foreign
College...................	23	47	26	18	40	36	61	59	16	31	33	42
Industrial arts...........	4	6	10	4	7	8	8	1	4	....	5	5
Commercial..............	15	15	18	17	19	18	.....	9	4	38	14	14
General.................	5	3	3	....	....	3	.....	1	8	8	4	2
Scientific................	53	29	43	61	34	35	31	30	68	23	44	37
Total.................	100	100	100	100	100	100	100	100	100	100	100	100
Number of cases	472	110	67	23	74	66	13	149	50	13	1,037	565

observed that the college course is much more and the scientific course much less popular among these boys than among those of native parentage. This tendency to choose the college course is especially strong among the immigrants from the south and east of Europe, including the Russian Jews. On the other hand, certain of the peoples from the north and west, notably the Scandinavians and the Germans and representatives of the British Empire in smaller measure, exhibit the American inclination toward the scientific course. It is difficult to give an explanation of these differences since both of these curricula are primarily college preparatory. Apparently some of these groups are captivated by the name, at least in so far as the boys are concerned.

BOYS AND GIRLS

It is well known that there are more girls than boys in the American high school, there being only about 85 boys to every 100 girls for the country as a whole. This greater tendency for the girls to attend high school, however, is not characteristic of all the immigrant groups. Examine Table XLIV in which the ratio of boys to girls is given for each of the groups.   Among those students whose fathers were born in the United States there are but 74.4 boys to every 100 girls.   In the case of the Italians, on the other hand, the ratio is 153.5, and the boys are in

TABLE XLIV

Number of Boys to 100 Girls in Bridgeport High School.   Students Grouped According to Nativity of Father.   Data from 2,257 Cases

Country of Father's Birth	No. Boys to 100 Girls
United States	74.4
Austria-Hungary	113.5
British Empire	76.1
Germany	82.1
Ireland	74.0
Italy	153.5
Poland	108.3
Russia	102.8
Scandinavia	86.2
All others	86.7
Total	85.0
All foreign	96.4

the majority in three other groups—the people of Austria-Hungary, the Poles, and the Russians.   Again is to be noted the cleavage between the north and west and the south and east of Europe.   The people from the former exhibit the American trait of sending the girls to high school, while those from the latter seemingly are less inclined to regard a secondary education as necessary for girls.

CHAPTER XIII

THE PUBLIC HIGH SCHOOL AND THE NEGRO

It is a well-known fact that the negroes do not patronize the secondary schools of the country in large numbers. The reports of the Commissioner of Education, in so far as they present separate data for negroes, indicate a large amount of retardation and relatively early elimination for the race as a whole. Commenting on this matter the Biennial Survey of Education for 1916–18 by the Bureau of Education makes the following summary statement: "In short, over seven times as great a proportion of white pupils as colored pupils are to be found in secondary schools of the South."

The causes of this situation are undoubtedly complex, reaching far back into the history and the nature of the negro. And no claim is put forward here of a complete explanation. Some interesting facts, however, have come to light that have at least some bearing on the question.

Since the number of negroes in Bridgeport, Mt. Vernon, and Seattle is negligible, no reference will be made in this chapter to data collected from these cities. St. Louis, on the other hand, as the population statistics already given show, does have a considerable negro population. Following the custom of the South this city maintains a dual system of education for the white and colored races, extending into the secondary field. One of the six St. Louis high schools, Sumner, is a negro high school. It is extraorinarily well attended, with an enrolment of over eight hundred. In fact, in proportion to the number residing in St. Louis, the negroes have as large an attendance in the public high schools as the whites. This is a remarkable showing, and it adds some interest to this part of the study.

Seven hundred and twenty-seven students in the high school filled out the information card. While this was not the total enrolment, it did include practically all who were present on the day this census was taken. The distribution of these young people according to sex and year in the high school is given in Table XLV. It will be observed that there are almost twice as many girls as boys. This seems to be characteristic of negroes generally, as it accords with the facts presented in the reports of the Bureau of Education and some other studies that have been made. As already noted, this is a cultural trait peculiar to the civilization of America and the north and west of Europe.

TABLE XLV

DISTRIBUTION BY SEX AND YEAR IN HIGH SCHOOL OF 727 STUDENTS IN THE SUMNER (COLORED) HIGH SCHOOL OF ST. LOUIS

Sex	Freshman	Sophomore	Junior	Senior	Total
Girls........	173	115	105	91	484
Boys........	102	66	32	43	243
Total....	275	181	137	134	727

FATHER'S OCCUPATION

Naturally these colored children would be expected to present an occupational representation quite different from that of the white children and characteristic of their race. Only slowly and against the most gigantic obstacles have the negroes been working their way upward through the several occupational levels since their emancipation from slavery less than three generations ago. At present the great majority of the members of this race in our cities are engaged in occupations requiring little skill. Their history has associated them with personal service. Since they own relatively little property few are found in those occupations which are based on its ownership, such as the proprietary and managerial callings. Furthermore, owing to a distinctly limited demand for professional service within the race, the number so engaged is small.

The occupations of the fathers of these 727 students are shown in Table XLVI. According to the facts here presented, as might be expected, personal service has the greatest representation, including 22 per cent, almost one-fourth of the total number. Common labor is second, and the machine trades third. It is perhaps surprising to find the clerical occupations occupying the fourth place, but this may be explained in terms of politics, since approximately three-fourths of them are mail clerks. Professional service is also represented in larger measure than might be expected. It should be remembered, however, that this type of service is not quite so rigid in its meaning as among the white population. Neither are the lines between occupations drawn so clearly. This fact is brought out by noting the composition of the several high-school years through data not presented in this table. The tendency noted again and again of certain of the occupational groups to maintain themselves in the high school is not apparent here. The proprietors and professionals, for example, are no better

TABLE XLVI

OCCUPATIONS OF THE FATHERS OF 727 STUDENTS IN THE SUMNER (COLORED) HIGH SCHOOL OF ST. LOUIS

Parental Occupation	Number	Percentage
Proprietors..........................	21	2.9
Professional service....................	48	6.6
Managerial service....................	38	5.2
Commercial service....................	11	1.5
Clerical service.......................	57	7.9
Agricultural service....................	30	4.1
Artisan-proprietors....................	28	3.8
Building trades.......................	24	3.3
Machine trades.......................	66	9.1
Printing trades.......................	2	.3
Miscellaneous trades...................	16	2.2
Transportation service.................	48	6.6
Public service........................	5	.7
Personal service......................	160	22.0
Miners, lumber-workers, fishermen.......	6	.8
Common labor........................	90	12.4
Unknown............................	77	10.6
Total............................	727	100.0

represented in the Senior than in the Freshman year. The only exception to the forgoing general statement is found in the case of common labor, which does exhibit the same traits as among the whites, but to a less marked degree.

FAMILY INFLUENCES

The negro family is not noted for its stability, and there are probably few factors of more importance in determining high-school attendance than the character of the family. Although it would be highly desirable to present data here dealing with the negro family in its varied aspects, this is not possible. Information was secured only on a few items. These, however, will be found to be significant.

The first and most important matter pertains to the mortality of the parents. Obviously the death of one of the parents is a most serious matter in the life of the child, particularly among those classes of the population whose standard of living approximates the margin of existence. In Table XLVII the facts for the students attending the Sumner

High School are compared with those for the students attending the other St. Louis high schools. And in Figure 34 the totals for the negro and white children are contrasted. According to the facts presented in this table 27.9 per cent of the negro children come from homes in which one or both parents are dead. This is more than one in every four students and is over twice the rate for the children of white parentage. The difference between the two races is more marked in the loss of the

TABLE XLVII

PERCENTAGE OF STUDENTS IN THE COLORED AND WHITE HIGH SCHOOLS OF ST. LOUIS
HAVING ONE OR BOTH PARENTS DECEASED

High School	Father Deceased	Mother Deceased	Both Parents Deceased	Total
Sumner High School (colored)........	12.8	10.0	5.1	27.9
Other St. Louis high schools (white)	7.6	3.8	1.3	12.7

mother than in the loss of the father; while the greatest contrast is seen in the loss of both parents, the rate for the negroes here being four times that for the whites. The high mortality rate among the negroes has long been noted. It is probably a function of their standard of living and mode of life. But its bearing on educational opportunity

Negro   (27.9)

White   (12.7)

FIG. 34.—Comparing the negro and white high-school students in St. Louis with respect to the percentage having one or both parents deceased.

has not received adequate recognition. Clearly this is an important consideration in a social order where large responsibilities for the education of the children still rest on the home.

Another significant measure of the integrity of the home is found in the occupation of the mother. Is the mother helping to support the family by working at some form of remunerative employment outside the home? Here again, in Figure 35, the negro and white students in the St. Louis high schools are compared. And, again, the unfavorable position of the former is noted. Over 30 per cent of the negro mothers are helping to support the family, whereas only 5.6 per cent of the mothers of the white children are so engaged. As a matter of fact, no occupational group among the latter even approches the negroes in this matter. As might be expected, the common laborers present a record nearest that of the negroes, but even here only 13 per cent of the mothers are helping to support the family.

Negro   (30.3)

White   (5.6)

FIG. 35.—Showing percentage of negro and white children in St. Louis high schools whose mothers are engaged in remunerative employment.

The size of the family from which the high-school students come is almost the same for the two races, if we think in terms of medians. For the negroes the median number of children in the family is 3.1; for the whites it is 2.8. The distribution of the size of the family for the two races, however, is somewhat different, as is shown in Figure 36.

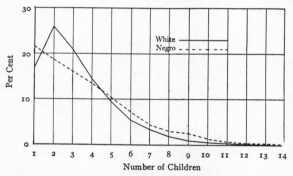

FIG. 36.—Comparing whites and negroes with respect to size of family from which the high-school students come. St. Louis.

The curve for the negroes is a peculiar one. It shows the most frequent number of children per family to be one. Whether this curve is characteristic of the negroes in St. Louis or to be explained in terms of the operation of a selective principle in the high-school population, it is impossible to say.

CHOICE OF CURRICULA

The children in the Sumner High School are offered practically the same choice of curricula as the children in the other St. Louis high schools. In view of the difference already noted in the social composition and occupational outlook of the two races, it would be natural to expect the negro children to exhibit distinctive traits in the selection of courses. It will be interesting to survey the facts.

Table XLVIII presents the curricular choices of the 484 negro girls in comparison with corresponding data from 3,978 girls of white parentage. The facts are given in percentages to make the comparison easy. An examination of the table will show that there are just two points at which the two races exhibit sharp differences. In the first place, the four-year home economics course appears to be actually

TABLE XLVIII

PERCENTAGE OF GIRL STUDENTS IN THE COLORED AND WHITE
HIGH SCHOOLS OF ST. LOUIS PURSUING THE
DIFFERENT CURRICULA

Curriculum	Negro	White
Four-year general	43.4	44.1
Four-year scientific	.6	.6
Four-year commercial	23.6	21.6
Four-year home economics	30.4	9.5
Four-year classical		1.0
Four-year fine arts	1.6	3.6
Two-year commercial	.4	18.5
Two-year home economics		.4
One-year commercial		.7
Total	100.0	100.0

popular among these colored girls, over 30 per cent of them taking it. This is the only group discovered in the four cities that seems to be interested in this course. It might be explained on the grounds that these girls are preparing for personal service, but data to be presented later indicate that only one of the 484 girls displays any intention of entering this occupation following graduation from high school. In the second place, the two-year commercial course is distinctly unpopular among these girls. Among the girls of white parentage, on the other hand, this course draws more students than any other course during the first and second years, except the general course, which points particularly to college. This difference may be due in part to inferior opportunities to enter into the clerical occupations on the part of colored girls. Perhaps, after all, the surprising thing about the facts presented in this table is that both races register practically the same proportion of

the girls in the general course.   This indicates a strong college tradition
in the Sumner High School, as well as in the other high schools of the
city.

Among the boys the differences are more pronounced than among
the girls, as a glance at Table XLIX will prove.   This is somewhat
surprising because, among the whites, the girls appear to be more bound
by the occupational group from which they come than are the boys.

TABLE XLIX

PERCENTAGE OF BOY STUDENTS IN THE COLORED AND WHITE
HIGH SCHOOLS OF ST. LOUIS PURSUING THE
DIFFERENT CURRICULA

Curriculum	Negro	White
Four-year general...............	14.0	42.1
Four-year scientific..............	9.5	9.4
Four-year commercial............	20.2	12.2
Four-year manual training........	54.7	23.9
Four-year classical..............	....	.8
Four-year fine arts..............	1.2	1.2
Two-year commercial............	.4	5.3
Two-year manual training........	....	4.7
Two-year printing...............	....	.3
One-year commercial............	....	.1
Total......................	100.0	100.0

There the boys tend to break over the class lines, while the girls conform
to them.   Only a small percentage of the colored boys are pursuing the
general curriculum, in which are enrolled 42 per cent of the white boys.
The four-year manual training course, on the other hand, is extremely
popular with the negroes.   Almost 55 per cent of them are taking it.
The four-year commercial course is also much more popular among them
than among the whites.   The various short courses appeal to the boys
of neither race.

EXPECTATIONS FOLLOWING GRADUATION

Perhaps just as significant as the curriculum chosen, if not more so,
is the statement of expectations of the students following graduation.
To be sure, little weight can be attached to these statements as indexes
of what these boys and girls will actually do when they leave the high
school.   In truth, the evidence is quite strong in the other direction,
namely, that many of them will not do that which they say they will do.
But, as an index of the traditions and atmosphere of the school, these
statements undoubtedly have weight.

A glance at Table L shows quite conclusively that at least according to their statements the negro girls are not intending to enter the occupations in which their parents are engaged. Apparently they plan to attend college in proportionately larger numbers than do their white sisters. They are likewise attracted to the normal school in such numbers as to set at rest any fear among the champions of education lest the colored schools be closed for lack of teachers. It should also be

TABLE L

EXPECTATIONS FOLLOWING GRADUATION OF GIRLS IN THE
COLORED AND WHITE HIGH SCHOOLS OF ST. LOUIS

Expectations	Negro	White
College..........................	35.3	33.7
Normal school	26.2	3.7
Business college................	2.1	4.2
Other school...................	3.9	1.6
Travel..........................	....	.1
Home...........................	....	1.6
Professional service.............	13.5	4.9
Commercial service.............	.2	.3
Clerical service.................	11.6	30.3
Industrial service...............	1.5	.5
Personal service................	.2	....
Work...........................	2.4	4.3
Undecided.....................	3.1	14.8
Total percentage............	100.0	100.0

noted that many of those mentioning the college as their immediate objective, intend ultimately to enter the teaching profession. And the 13.5 per cent grouped under professional service includes a large proportion who are expecting to begin teaching with only the high-school training. Clearly teaching is attractive to these young people. The profession still retains the prestige which it has lost among members of the other race. A summary inspection of the table shows that the occupational interest which dominates this group of negro girls is the professional, and that they are hoping the high school will provide a means of escape from the wage-earning class from which they come and back to which most of them will probably have to go.

The negro boys also are intent on a higher education. This is seen in Table LI. According to their statements 63 per cent of these boys are planning to attend college. This is almost 12 per cent greater than for the boys of white parentage. A second interesting feature of the table is the relatively large proportion of colored boys looking toward the industrial occupations.   But this is absolutely quite small, amounting to only 8.7 per cent.   A third point of interest is the smaller proportion of negroes who are undecided.   A glance at the preceding table shows this to be true of the girls as well as the boys.

In conclusion it may be said that this brief and somewhat superficial study of the population of a single negro high school throws some light on the relation of the negro to our secondary schools.   His relative

TABLE LI

EXPECTATIONS FOLLOWING GRADUATION OF BOYS IN THE
COLORED AND WHITE HIGH SCHOOLS OF ST. LOUIS

Expectations	Negro	White
College........................	63.0	51.4
Business college.................	....	.5
Other school	4.6	2.2
Travel.........................	.4	.1
Farming........................	.4	.4
Professional service..............	1.2	1.0
Commercial service..............	.8	3.2
Clerical service	5.3	5.5
Industrial service................	8.7	2.6
Public service...................	....	.1
Personal service.................	.8	....
Transportation service	....	.3
Work...........................	7.8	16.7
Undecided......................	7.0	16.0
Total percentage	100.0	100.0

absence of interest in the high school is rather easy to understand. As a race the negroes are engaged in occupations which require little skill, for which the remuneration is low, and whose respectability is not high.   Their standard of living is also low, and the home is not the center of stimulation and inspiration that it is among other groups in the population.   The family is notoriously unstable because of the absence of those traditions that would give it stability.   The high mortality of the race also acts as a disorganizing and disintegrating force in many negro homes.   Taking into consideration these various influences, the attendance at the Sumner High School in St. Louis is little short of marvelous.   These young people are carrying on a struggle for secondary education that is really unique in the annals of American education.   The obvious handicaps under which they are striving can be duplicated by few social groups in this country today outside their own race.   The present study shows no group within the white population in the four cities investigated waging the fight so successfully and against such tremendous odds, as is the negro population of St. Louis. Those elements of the white population that might be regarded as approximating the negroes in standard of living, social tradition, and the general organization of life are very far from doing as well. The children from these groups hardly get into the high school at all. It is very doubtful if, outside the negro populations of a very few of the large cities midway between the north and south, such as Washington, there is any population group within the nation that is doing so much to send its children to high school as are the negroes of St. Louis.

CHAPTER XIV

THE PUBLIC HIGH SCHOOL AND PSYCHOLOGICAL SELECTION

It has been made clear in the earlier chapters that the student population of the public high school is sociologically highly selected. It remains to consider briefly the question of psychological selection— briefly because this does not constitute the central part of the study and because much has been done in this field in recent years.

Psychological tests were given to the four groups of children in Bridgeport and to the students in the first year of the high school in Mt. Vernon. In the former city the Chapman-Welles Junior and Senior High School Classification Test was used and in the latter the National Intelligence Tests, Scale B, Form 1. We shall now examine the data secured from these two cities, giving special attention to the data from Bridgeport, because of the more comprehensive study made there.

CHILDREN OF HIGH-SCHOOL AGE IN HIGH SCHOOL AND OUT

The median scores made by the girls and boys in each of the high-school years in Bridgeport are given in Table LII. Although the facts in this table, apart from a comparison with data from the other groups

TABLE LII

MEDIAN SCORES MADE BY GIRLS AND BOYS IN EACH YEAR OF THE HIGH SCHOOL IN BRIDGEPORT—CHAPMAN-WELLES TEST. DATA FROM 2,537 CASES

High-School Year	Girls	Boys
Freshman	72.9	89.7
Sophomore	90.8	101.8
Junior	95.4	110.7
Senior	99.2	113.8
Number of cases	1,362	1,175

studied in this city, are of no great significance to this study, there are several points of interest to be noted. The median score increases noticeably in the succsessive years of the high school, yet for both sexes the most pronounced difference occurs between the Freshman and Sophomore years. This may be due to disproportionate elimination at this point in the high school, but more probably to the fact that the test is not well adapted to measuring differences among the more mature students in the later high-school years. It is also observed that the median score for the boys is in each case appreciably higher than that for the girls. It seems probable that this is likewise to be explained in terms of the organization of the test.

But it is the comparison with these other groups of children of high-school age that interests us. These comparative scores are presented in Table LIII. No score is given for the girls in the first year of

TABLE LIII

MEDIAN SCORES MADE BY GIRLS AND BOYS IN THE FIRST YEAR OF THE HIGH SCHOOL, THE EVENING HIGH SCHOOL, THE FIRST YEAR OF THE TRADE SCHOOL, AND THE COMPULSORY CONTINUATION CLASSES IN BRIDGEPORT—CHAPMAN-WELLES TEST

Group	Girls	Boys	Number of Cases
First year high school.................	72.9	89.7	910
Evening high school..................	60.0	78.1	181
First year trade school...............	....	62.0	112
Continuation classes.................	29.1	40.9	421

the trade school because the number of cases was entirely too small to insure reliability. The outstanding fact in the table is that, speaking in terms of medians, the children in the Freshman year of the high school are distinctly superior to those in the other groups. And in the case of

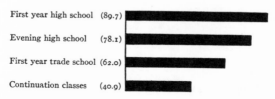

First year high school   (89.7)

Evening high school   (78.1)

First year trade school   (62.0)

Continuation classes   (40.9)

FIG. 37.—Showing the median score made in the Chapman-Welles Test by the boys in each of four groups. Bridgeport.

the evening high school the difference is more significant than these scores indicate, because these students are on the average two to three years older than those in the first year of the high school. In Figure 37 a graphical comparison is made of the median scores for the boys in these four groups. No comment is necessary.

Median scores, however, tell but a part of the truth. For this reason Figure 38 was constructed, in which is presented the complete distribution of the scores made by each of three groups of boys, those in the first year of the high school, those in the first year of the trade school, and those in the compulsory continuation classes. The boys in these three groups are of approximately the same age. Observe the character of the curves. The curve for the high-school Freshmen

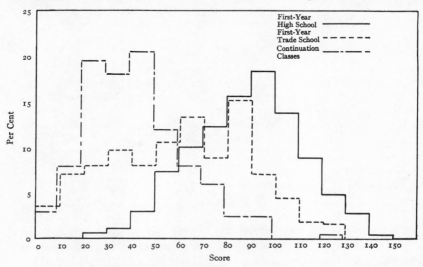

FIG. 38.—Showing by percentages the distribution of scores made by each of three groups of boys in the Chapman-Welles Test. Data from 426 boys in the first year of the high school, 112 boys in the first year of the trade school, and 201 boys in the compulsory continuation classes. Bridgeport.

shows a fairly normal distribution about a center of superior ability, while that for the continuation classes exhibits a similar distribution about a center of mediocre or inferior ability. On the other hand, the curve for the first year of the trade school shows a wide and somewhat irregular distribution. The first two curves are to be expected, but why this peculiar distribution for the trade school? The probable explanation is to be found in the educational status of this institution and the attitude of school teachers and others toward it. There is no policy of admission that would close the doors of the trade school to children judged inferior by academic standards. In many instances, as a matter of fact, children who have failed in the conventional curriculum are encouraged to try this school. This accounts for the large number of cases at the lower end of the distribution, but it does not explain the presence of many children of average and even superior ability. Apparently they enter the trade school either through necessity or because of interest in, or an aptitude for, various types of manual activity.

Perhaps a word should be said about the overlapping of these curves. This is certainly just as significant as the fact of median differences. There is very large overlapping between the high-school and trade-school curves, and even the compulsory continuation classes hold a considerable area in common with the high school Freshmen. Although the children in these classes have in the main been rejected as unfit by the school, there is a surprisingly large amount of ability to be found among them. There are even a few of distinctly superior promise, at least as measured by this test. On the other hand, in the high school there are some children of remarkably inferior ability. Thus, while we may say that the high-school population represents a certain measure of psychological selection, it is clear that this principle does not operate conclusively in a negative fashion and much less in a positive way in determining attendance at high school. Neither are all of meager intellectual endowment barred from high school, nor are all possessing superior talent to be found within its doors.

There is another point of interest in the data from the trade school that deserves some comment. The boys in the second year not only did not do as well in the test as those in the first year, but they actually made a median record almost ten points lower. As already given in the table, the median for the first year is 62.0, while that for the second year is but 52.9; and it should be noted further that there is a median age difference of 1.3 years in favor of the second-year boys. While no sweeping conclusions may be drawn from data from a single school, these facts give rise to the suspicion that the work of the trade school is not of such a character as to demand ability of the type measured by this and similar tests.

CHOICE OF CURRICULA

That a certain amount of psychological selection is expressed in the choice of curricula is to be expected. The extent to which this occurs in the Bridgeport High School is shown in Table LIV. Here are given the median scores made by both boys and girls pursuing the various curricula in each year of the high school. Data are presented for but three curricula for each sex, because of the very small number of students to be found in the other curricula offered. Examination of that part of the table presenting the facts for the girls reveals appreciable differences. Averaging the medians for the four years we get a record for the girls in the college preparatory course of 95.9, as compared with 89.8 for those in the normal course and 86.8 for those in the commercial course. These differences are not large, and there is great overlapping of the distributions, but they do indicate some selection.

TABLE LIV

Median Scores Made by Girls and Boys in the Various Curricula in the Bridgeport High School—Chapman-Welles Test

Curriculum	Freshman	Sophomore	Junior	Senior	Average	No. Cases
	Girls					
College............	73.0	97.7	101.0	111.7	95.9	271
Normal............	75.4	87.0	95.7	98.0	89.8	376
Commercial.......	71.8	89.4	91.6	94.4	86.8	715
Total.........	72.9	90.8	95.4	99.2	89.6	1,362
	Boys					
College...........	92.5	105.3	113.0	118.0	107.2	371
Scientific.........	86.3	100.8	114.6	111.5	103.3	556
Commercial.......	82.9	100.9	121.5	135.0	110.1	148
Total.........	89.7	101.8	110.7	113.8	108.7	1,075

Turning to the other half of the table, which gives the facts for the boys, we observe no consistent tendency for any one of the groups to show superiority from year to year. There are some average differences, but they are not significant. The absence of any definite selection here may be due to the fact that no one of these curricula is strictly vocational, although the commercial course approaches it. If the number in the industrial arts course were sufficiently large to furnish reliable medians, it is probable that some selection would be found among the boys.

In Mt. Vernon the National Intelligence Tests were given to the high-school Freshmen. The median scores made by both sexes in the different curricula are given in Table LV. The several academic curricula are grouped, and no data are given for the girls pursuing the industrial arts course because of an insufficient number of cases. It is at once apparent that in Mt. Vernon the academic curricula are attracting the students of superior ability regardless of sex, while the lowest record is made by the boys in the industrial arts course. Yet it should be noted that there is much overlapping, and that in the vocational courses there are many students of unusual talent.

TABLE LV

MEDIAN SCORES MADE BY FRESHMAN GIRLS AND BOYS IN EACH TYPE OF CURRICULUM IN THE MT. VERNON HIGH SCHOOL—NATIONAL INTELLIGENCE TESTS

CURRICULUM	GIRLS		BOYS	
	Median Score	No. of Cases	Median Score	No. of Cases
Academic.................	155.3	157	155.0	180
Commercial..............	144.1	85	147.5	67
Industrial arts	....	....	130.0	34

PARENTAL OCCUPATION

In Table LVI are given the scores made in the Chapman-Welles Test in the Bridgeport High School by the students grouped according to the occupation of the father, the boys and girls being kept separate

TABLE LVI

SCORES MADE BY GIRLS AND BOYS FROM DIFFERENT OCCUPATIONAL GROUPS IN THE CHAPMAN-WELLES TEST. IN EACH CASE THE MEDIAN SCORES MADE IN THE FOUR HIGH-SCHOOL YEARS ARE AVERAGED. DATA FROM BRIDGEPORT HIGH SCHOOL

PARENTAL OCCUPATION	GIRLS		BOYS	
	Average of Medians	No. of Cases	Average of Medians	No. of Cases
Proprietors......................	91.8	213	105.4	193
Professional service	103.3	66	104.8	59
Managerial service	94.5	191	109.4	161
Commercial service	94.3	77	110.5	71
Clerical service	95.8	55	107.7	31
Artisan-proprietors.	85.1	59	107.8	39
Buildings trades.................	91.3	54	103.7	47
Machine trades	92.3	161	107.3	131
Miscellaneous trades	84.8	74	107.9	51
Transportation service	84.8	36	112.5	28
Personal service	81.3	23	101.9	19
Common labor	90.0	16	95.0	17
All manual-labor occupations...	88.8	404	105.8	316
All occupations..............	91.6	1,128	106.9	898

because of the sex differences already noted. For each group the median scores for the four high-school years are averaged. Several of the occupational groups are omitted from this table because of inadequate representation in one or more years. For the purpose of focusing special attention on the laboring groups they are all combined into a single group at the bottom of the table. In this group are included the building, machine, printing, and miscellaneous trades, the transportation workers, public service, personal service, and common labor.

An examination of the table shows no clear differences. And the evidence from the separate years of the high school, not given here, supports this statement. Although for both the girls and the boys the combined labor groups do average a point or so lower than the entire high-school population, the difference is so small as to constitute an entirely insufficient basis on which to build sweeping conclusions. In

TABLE LVII

MEDIAN SCORES MADE BY FRESHMEN OF THE MT. VERNON HIGH SCHOOL IN THE NATIONAL INTELLIGENCE TESTS, CLASSIFIED ACCORDING TO THE OCCUPATION OF THE FATHER

Parental Occupation	Median Score	No. of Cases
Proprietors	147.9	50
Professional service	158.2	25
Managerial service	152.5	23
Commercial service	152.5	22
Clerical service	138.2	13
Artisan-proprietors	152.5	12
All laboring groups	141.5	48

Bridgeport at least the high-school students from the various occupational groups exhibit about the same measure of ability. This indicates again that the children of manual laborers who get into the high school are relatively highly selected, since the testing of an unselected group of children from this source shows an intelligence level appreciably lower than that of children from the professional and more prosperous classes.

In Mt. Vernon, however, we do find some differences in the small group in the Freshman class for whom we have all the necessary data. The facts are presented in Table LVII. In order to secure a sufficiently large number of cases for statistical purposes all the laboring groups are combined. If the record made by the children of this combination group is compared with records made by those whose fathers are engaged in other occupations, the comparison is found to be somewhat unfavorable to the laboring classes, although the clerical service does show a slightly lower record.   But even in Mt. Vernon the complete distributions show the differences to merit less attention than the points of agreement.

THE IMMIGRANT

The test records made by the high-school students in Bridgeport, classified according to the father's country of birth, appear in Table LVIII.   Since this table is organized in the same way as the previous table giving similar data for the occupational groups, no explanation is necessary.   If we compare the records made by the combined immigrant groups with those made by children of native parentage, they are found to be almost identical, the boys displaying slight superiority in the former and the girls in the latter group.   These differences are not large enough to enable us to say, however, that the immigrant boys are superior and the immigrant girls inferior to the American children in this high school. With the exception of the Italian and Polish children, whose records are considerably below the average for both sexes, the children of foreign parentage appear to hold their own very well.

TABLE LVIII

SCORES MADE IN CHAPMAN-WELLES TEST BY GIRLS AND BOYS, CLASSIFIED ACCORD-
ING TO NATIVITY OF THE FATHER.   MEDIAN SCORES MADE IN THE FOUR
SCHOOL YEARS ARE AVERAGED IN EACH CASE—BRIDGEPORT HIGH SCHOOL

Country of Father's Birth	GIRLS		BOYS	
	Average of Medians	No. of Cases	Average of Medians	No. of Cases
United States............	92.5	586	106.7	405
Austria-Hungary..........	84.1	93	109.2	97
British Empire...........	92.1	82	108.7	57
Germany.................	86.0	27	111.9	19
Ireland.................	90.3	98	100.5	66
Italy...................	80.0	39	99.0	55
Poland..................	83.8	8	99.4	10
Russia..................	91.8	135	109.2	132
Scandinavia.............	93.9	51	106.3	49
All foreign countries...	90.6	644	107.1	493

A similar situation is found among the Freshmen in the Mt. Vernon High School.   Since the number of children of immigrant stock is small, they are all included in a single group.   This gives us for the girls of native and foreign parentage the median scores of 155.5 and 151.3 respectively.   The corresponding scores for the boys are 156.2 and

154.0. There is in each case a slight difference favoring the former, but hardly large enough to deserve comment. We may say, therefore, that, regardless of any differences in ability that may be found in unselected groups of children from the native and various immigrant stocks, such differences are practically obscure in the high-school population.

FAMILY INFLUENCES

A study of the records made in the tests by the firstborn and lastborn in families of two or more children brings to light evidence which supports the conclusions in an earlier chapter that selective influences are operating at this point. In Table LIX are compared the scores made in the Chapman-Welles Test by the firstborn and lastborn children in the Bridgeport High School. As in previous tables, in order to get a single measure for each group the median scores made by the students in the four years are averaged. For both the boys and the girls, it will be observed, the firstborn make a score significantly larger than that made by the lastborn children.

TABLE LIX

COMPARISON OF SCORES MADE BY FIRSTBORN AND LASTBORN CHILDREN IN THE BRIDGEPORT HIGH SCHOOL IN THE CHAPMAN-WELLES TEST. IN EACH CASE THE MEDIAN SCORES MADE IN THE FOUR HIGH-SCHOOL YEARS ARE AVERAGED

Order of Birth	GIRLS		BOYS	
	Average of Medians	No. of Cases	Average of Medians	No. of Cases
Firstborn...............	94.8	287	108.3	264
Lastborn...............	87.8	247	102.8	205

Among the Freshmen of the Mt. Vernon High School the same relation is found, as an examination of Table LX will show. What is the explanation? Certainly not that firstborn are brighter than lastborn children, but rather that the former in the high school are more highly selected groups than the latter. Among certain elements of the population the firstborn child is more likely to be called on to sacrifice his own educational opportunities in the interests of the family than is the lastborn. Especially, if he does not possess unusual ability, it seems that he will receive less encouragement than his younger brother or sister to remain in school. In other words, that general tendency of the high school to select children of superior talent and reject others operates with peculiar force among the firstborn, because of the influence of certain sociological factors.

TABLE LX

COMPARISON OF MEDIAN SCORES MADE IN THE NATIONAL INTELLIGENCE TESTS BY FIRSTBORN AND LASTBORN CHILDREN IN THE MT. VERNON HIGH SCHOOL

Order of Birth	GIRLS		BOYS	
	Median Score	No. of Cases	Median Score	No. of Cases
Firstborn...............	151.3	27	154.2	38
Lastborn...............	147.5	22	146.7	24

It is also interesting to note the relation of ability to the number of children in the family, keeping in mind of course that the validity of these tests is assumed. The facts from the Bridgeport High School are presented in Table LXI. It will be observed that the students are classified into three groups on the basis of the number of children in the family from which they come. First, there is the family with an only child; second, the family with from two to four children; and third, the family with five or more children. According to this table the score seems to vary inversely with the size of the family for both the girls and the boys.

TABLE LXI

COMPARISON OF SCORES MADE IN CHAPMAN-WELLES TEST BY CHILDREN COMING FROM FAMILIES OF THREE DIFFERENT SIZES IN THE BRIDGEPORT HIGH SCHOOL. IN EACH CASE THE MEDIAN SCORES MADE IN THE FOUR HIGH-SCHOOL YEARS ARE AVERAGED

NUMBER OF CHILDREN IN THE FAMILY	GIRLS		BOYS	
	Average of Medians	No. of Cases	Average of Medians	No. of Cases
1......................	94.2	118	113.6	112
2-4....................	92.6	599	107.0	523
5+....................	89.3	308	104.2	263

Data bearing on this same point from Mt. Vernon appear in Table LXII. The evidence here corroborates the findings in Bridgeport. Apparently the superior children exist in proportionately larger numbers in the smaller families. But the explanation is probably to be found in the voluntary limitation of the birth-rate among the more intelligent and foresighted elements of the population. The ultimate

TABLE LXII

COMPARISON OF MEDIAN SCORES MADE IN THE NATIONAL INTELLIGENCE TESTS BY CHILDREN COMING FROM FAMILIES OF THREE DIFFERENT SIZES IN THE MT. VERNON HIGH SCHOOL

No. of Children in the Family	Girls		Boys	
	Median Score	No. of Cases	Median Score	No. of Cases
1	148.8	9	165.0	8
2–4	146.7	62	151.4	63
5+	139.2	19	139.6	39

effect of such a policy on the soundness and quality of the racial stock is obvious, but a discussion of this matter is beyond the scope of this study.

CHAPTER XV

THE POPULATION OF THE PRIVATE SECONDARY SCHOOL

There are in the United States 158,745 students enrolled in the private secondary schools, according to the report of the Federal Bureau for the school year 1917–18. While the proportion of the total secondary-school population to be found in these schools has been decreasing gradually for fifty years and probably for an even longer period, the number is still sufficiently large to receive attention in any study of this character. This chapter may, therefore, be regarded as a supplement to the more detailed study of the social composition of the public high-school population reported in the preceding chapters. It will throw additional light on the extension of the opportunities of secondary education to the various strata of American society.

But there is a second consideration that lends significance to this part of the study. It has been remarked that in the primitive peoples inhabiting various parts of the globe today we may see our contemporaneous ancestors. While this construction must not be taken literally, since each people, even the most primitive, has experienced a longer or shorter period of evolution that has produced certain unique and special characteristics, it does contain a certain element of truth. So in the private secondary schools of today we see preserved some of those features which characterized the secondary institutions of a few generations ago, before the rise of the public high school. By comparing the high-school population with that of the private secondary schools we may, therefore, get some idea of the distance we have traveled in actual practice from the conception of secondary education as class education. Of course there are certain forces operating today to determine the character of the population of these private schools which did not affect the schools of the earlier period, but in general the impression made by the comparison probably corresponds with the facts. The elements in the population which patronize the private secondary schools today in all probability gave their children a secondary education in the days when it was not free and when it looked toward the college altogether. To be sure, a considerable number of parents who do not patronize the private secondary schools would send their children to these schools today if there were no public schools of secondary grade, but it is not probable that these additions would greatly change the social complexion of the student population there enrolled.

Data were secured from two schools: the one, a day school in the Middle West, and the other, a famous boarding-school in New England. They are respectively the University of Chicago High School in Chicago, Illinois, and the Phillips-Exeter Academy at Exeter, New Hampshire.

Owing to the very rapid development of Roman Catholic secondary schools during the last twenty years, an effort was made to secure the facts from one of these schools, but without success. The administrative officers approached seemed not to be interested in a study of this character.

Perhaps a few words should be set down concerning the nature of the two schools studied. Exeter Academy is a non-sectarian school offering

TABLE LXIII

OCCUPATIONS OF FATHERS OR GUARDIANS OF 201 STUDENTS IN PHILLIPS-EXETER ACADEMY AND 418 IN THE UNIVERSITY OF CHICAGO HIGH SCHOOL

PARENTAL OCCUPATION	EXETER ACADEMY		U. OF C. HIGH SCHOOL		TOTAL	
	Number	Percentage	Number	Percentage	Number	Percentage
Proprietors..............	88	44.0	176	42.1	264	42.7
Professional service......	62	31.0	130	31.1	192	31.0
Managerial service.......	21	10.5	50	12.0	71	11.5
Commercial service.......	15	7.5	41	9.8	56	9.0
Clerical service..........	5	2.5	8	1.9	13	2.1
Artisan-proprietors.......	3	1.5	5	1.2	8	1.3
Agricultural service.......	2	1.0	2	.5	4	.7
Manual labor............	2	1.0	......	....	2	.3
Unknown................	3	1.0	6	1.4	9	1.4
Total..............	201	100.0	418	100.0	619	100.0

a four-year academic course and enrolling about 575 students, all of whom are boys. The University of Chicago High School is coeducational and non-sectarian and is definitely college preparatory. Its registration is about 475. Both schools have tuition fees, that of the former being $200 and that of the latter $275. In addition to the tuition fee at Exeter there are the annual charges for room and board and other assessments which range from $336 to $1,091, according to the catalogue for 1920–21.

Data were not secured from the entire population in either school, since it was felt that a random sampling would be sufficient for our purposes.   As shown in Table LXIII returns were received from 201 students in Exeter and 418 in the University of Chicago High School.

THE PARENTAL OCCUPATION

As in the study of the public high school, the most significant thing here is the occupation of the parent or guardian.   The facts for the two schools are presented in Table LXIII.   A glance at this table makes it clear that the social composition of the student population in these

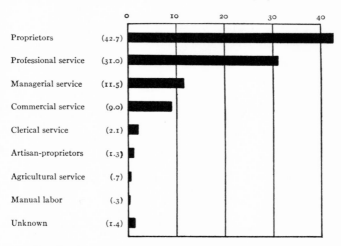

FIG. 39.—Showing by percentages the occupations of the fathers or guardians of 619 students in Phillips-Exeter Academy and the University of Chicago High School.   June, 1921.

schools is decidedly different from that of the public high-school population.   And, furthermore, Phillips-Exeter Academy and the University of Chicago High School draw their students from almost exactly the same elements in the population.   About the only difference worthy of mention is the slightly larger representation of the managerial and commercial workers in the latter and a correspondingly greater percentage of proprietors and clerical workers in the former.

The percentages for the two schools combined are presented graphically in Figure 39.   It will be observed that the proprietors have the largest representation, with 42.7 per cent of the students.   Then follows the professional service with 31.0 per cent. No other group can be said to be well represented in these schools. Consequently it may be said that private secondary schools of the more exclusive type are organized practically for these two classes in the population. The relatively poor representation of the managerial service is perhaps surprising until it is recalled that quite a large proportion of the purely managerial positions are not high-grade positions and that many of the individuals holding these positions have been promoted from some form of skilled labor. Considering their numbers in the population the commercial workers have a fair representation, while the clerical workers are almost wholly absent. There are very few artisan-proprietors and farmers; and the many grades and varieties of manual labor combined account for only .3 per cent of the total enrolment of the two schools. It is probable that more detailed and comprehensive knowledge of these few cases would reveal the influence of certain special circumstances not ordinarily associated with manual labor.

It is interesting at this point to make a comparison with the public high-school population. This is done in Table LXIV. According to

TABLE LXIV

Occupations of Fathers or Guardians of 17,265 Students in the Public High Schools of Bridgeport, Mt. Vernon, St. Louis, and Seattle, and 619 Students in the Phillips-Exeter Academy and the University of Chicago High School

Parental Occupation	High Schools of Bridgeport, Mt. Vernon, St. Louis, Seattle	Phillips-Exeter Academy and University of Chicago High School
Proprietors	19.8	42.7
Professional service	9.4	31.0
Managerial service	16.5	11.5
Commercial service	9.5	9.0
Clerical service	5.8	2.1
Artisan-proprietors	4.2	1.3
Agricultural service	2.4	.7
Manual labor	29.1	.3
Unknown	3.3	1.4
Total	100.0	100.0

this table only two occupational groups have a greater proportional representation in the private than in the public secondary schools—the professional service and the proprietors. All the rest are less well represented, although only slightly so in the case of the commerical service. Then follow the managerial service, the clerical service, the artisan-proprietors, the agricultural service, and finally manual labor. It is in this last group that the most pronounced difference is to be found. While 29.1 per cent of all the students in the public high schools come from the laboring classes, only a negligible proportion of those in these private schools are from this source. Thus, while public secondary education in the United States is still highly selective, it is certainly much less so than private. And, assuming that these private schools do give us a relatively reliable picture of the social composition of our secondary-school population of a few generations ago, it is clear that we have traveled a considerable distance from the conception of secondary education as class education.

NATIVITY OF THE FATHER

The students in these two schools are very largely of American parentage. This is shown in Table LXV in which they are classified

TABLE LXV

NATIVITY OF FATHERS OF 619 STUDENTS IN THE PHILLIPS-EXETER ACADEMY AND THE UNIVERSITY OF CHICAGO HIGH SCHOOL

Country of Father's Birth	Number	Percentage
United States....................	540	87.3
Austria-Hungary................	6	1.0
British Empire..................	41	6.6
France.........................	4	.6
Germany........................	17	2.7
Ireland........................	3	.5
Italy..........................	1	.2
Russia.........................	3	.5
Scandinavia....................	2	.3
All others	2	.3
Total.....................	619	100.0

according to the nativity of the father. In the two schools combined 87.3 per cent of the fathers of the students were born in this country, and over one-half of the remainder were born in English-speaking countries. It will be noticed further that the south and east of Europe are practically without representation. These schools draw from the native stock and the peoples from the north and west of Europe.

NUMBER OF BROTHERS AND SISTERS

In view of the foregoing facts concerning occupation and nativity it is to be expected that the families from which these children come should be somewhat smaller than those from which the public high school is recruited. And such is the case to a small degree, as may be seen by examining Table LXVI. According to this table the median number of brothers and sisters is higher for the students in the public high schools in each of the cities than it is for those in either of the private schools. This figure is lowest in the University of Chicago High School, where it is but 1.3, and highest in the Bridgeport High School, where it reaches 2.3.

TABLE LXVI

MEDIAN NUMBER OF BROTHERS AND SISTERS OF THE STUDENTS IN THE PUBLIC HIGH SCHOOLS OF FOUR CITIES AND IN TWO PRIVATE SECONDARY SCHOOLS

Secondary Schools	Median Number Brothers and Sisters
Bridgeport	2.3
Mt. Vernon	2.1
Seattle	2.0
St. Louis	1.8
Exeter Academy	1.7
University of Chicago High School	1.3

In conclusion it should be pointed out that the differences between the public high school and these private secondary schools are actually greater than statistics indicate. In all probability, for example, there is an important average difference between the managerial service represented in the two types of schools. Fathers engaged in these occupations who send their children to the private school hold positions somewhat superior as a rule to those held by fathers similarly classed who send their children to the public schools. Many of those representing the managerial occupations in the high school are foremen while this grade is practically absent in the private school. The same may be said of each of the remaining occupational groups, when examined in the concrete. Thus we may conclude that, while the public high school is still a class institution in a very real sense, yet the great increase in the secondary-school population of the last forty years marks a considerable advance toward the democratization of secondary education.

PART III. CONCLUSION AND INTERPRETATION

CHAPTER XVI

THE SELECTIVE CHARACTER OF AMERICAN
SECONDARY EDUCATION

In view of the foregoing analysis it is clear that we in America have not abandoned in practice the selective principle in secondary education, even though we have established a free public high school in almost every community in the country. It is not strictly in accord with the facts to say that "a public high school differs from an elementary school chiefly in the age of its children." It is true that children in high school are on the average somewhat older than those in the elementary school, yet, as a matter of fact, there is not very much difference in the ages of pupils enrolled in the eighth grade and those in the first year of the high school. High-school students, even today and in spite of the amazing growth of the high-school enrolment since 1880, are a highly selected group. And this difference is just as important as the difference in age. Secondary education is not education for adolescence, as elementary education is education for childhood, but rather education for a selected group of adolescents, as we have seen in the preceding chapters, and as we shall note again now in summary.

PARENTAL OCCUPATION AND THE PUBLIC HIGH SCHOOL

There is a close relation between parental occupation and the privileges of secondary education. If we examine the entire high-school population, we find certain occupational groups very well and others very poorly represented, in proportion to their numbers in the general population. Among the former are the five great non-labor groups with professional service occupying the most advantageous position, followed by the proprietors, commercial service, managerial service, and clerical service. At the other end of the series are the lower grades of labor with common labor almost unrepresented and personal service, miners, lumber-workers, and fishermen, and the miscellaneous trades and machine operatives in the manufacturing and mechanical industries, occupying somewhat better positions in the order named. The other occupational groups are found between these two extremes. Next to the non-labor groups are the printing trades and the public service, followed by the machine trades, transportation service, and the building trades. In general, the order here given reflects the social and economic status of the occupation, its educational and intellectual standards, and the stability of employment.

Not only do these various occupational classes exhibit different degrees of representation in the high school at the beginning of the course, but those very groups that are under-represented in the Freshman year have the smallest ratio of Seniors to Freshmen. In fact, the representation of an occupation in the first year of the high school is at the same time a fairly accurate measure of its tendency to persist through the fourth year. Consequently, the differences among the groups become more and more pronounced in the successive years of the school. The student population gradually becomes more and more homogeneous as the source from which it is drawn becomes more narrow, until by the time the Senior year of the high school is reached, the student body exhibits a distinctly class character. Here the representatives of the laboring classes are few indeed in proportion to their number in the general population, and the lower grades of labor have practically disappeared. This is brought out in striking fashion by the data from Mt. Vernon in which the sixth grade is contrasted with the last year of the high school.

Evidence in corroboration of these conclusions, drawn from a study of the high-school population, is derived from the investigation of groups of children of high-school age not in high school in Seattle and Bridgeport. In the former city, a study of 514 children of high-school age at work showed a social composition very different from that of the high-school population. Here, four great labor groups—the building trades, common labor, machine trades, and transportation service—contribute over 60 per cent of the children. The situation is just the reverse of that found in the high school. In Bridgeport a similar condition is found. In the evening high school of that city the sons and daughters of the laboring classes constitute the great majority of the enrolment with the machine trades in the lead, followed by the miscellaneous trades, common labor, and the building trades. In the trade school the situation is about the same except that the representation of the laboring classes is yet larger and common labor forges ahead of the miscellaneous trades to second place. Apparently the children of the laboring classes are destined to follow in the footsteps of their fathers. This representation of the labor groups is still further increased in that group of educational unfortunates enrolled in the compulsory continuation classes in which common labor holds first place, accounting for over one-fourth of the entire registration.

These differences in the extent of educational opportunity are further accentuated through the choice of curricula. As a rule, those groups which are poorly represented in the high school patronize the more narrow and practical curricula, the curricula which stand as terminal points in the educational system and which prepare for wage-earning. And the poorer their representation in high school, the greater is the probability that they will enter these curricula. The one- and two-year vocational courses, wherever offered, draw their registration particularly, from the ranks of labor. This tendency is considerably more pronounced among the girls than among the boys. The former seem to be peculiarly bound by the social class from which they come. One is surprised at the unmistakable class character of the girls' college preparatory course in a high school such as that in Bridgeport. Furthermore, the thesis may be cautiously advanced that these differences appear somewhat more clearly in the East than in the West, but it is hardly safe to generalize on the basis of returns from four cities.

A study of expectations following graduation, as given by the students, indicates that this selective principle continues to operate beyond the period of secondary education. Those classes which are least well represented in the last year of the high school will apparently be yet less well represented in the colleges and universities. And, as in the case of the choice of curricula, this tendency is more marked among the girls than among the boys, in the East than in the West.

THE PUBLIC HIGH SCHOOL AND THE CULTURAL LEVEL

Parental occupation, as one index of cultural level, exhibits a close relation to educational opportunity. The same is true of the possession of a telephone in the home, according to the returns from Bridgeport and Mt. Vernon. In the former city, it was found that telephones are two and one-half times as frequent in the homes of high-school students as in those of children attending the trade school, and seven times as frequent as in the homes of the children in the compulsory continuation classes. Furthermore, the percentage of telephones increases decidedly from year to year in the high school. Thus we find but 39.7 per cent of the students in the Freshman year coming from homes with telephones, whereas in the Senior year, this percentage is 60.3. There are also wide differences among the curricula in this respect. In the case of the girls, telephones are almost twice as frequent in the homes of those who are enrolled in the college preparatory as in the homes of those taking the commercial course. And these curricular differences are less marked among the boys than among the girls as was observed in the study of the parental occupation. Data from Mt. Vernon, including returns from the sixth grade, support in every particular these conclusions drawn from the Bridgeport study.

THE PUBLIC HIGH SCHOOL AND FAMILY INFLUENCES

All the evidence brought to light in this study points to the importance of the family as a powerful factor in determining attendance at high school. The mortality of parents of high-school students is found to be considerably below the expectation for children of high-school age, and does not increase perceptibly from the Freshman to the Senior year. In fact, according to the returns from Mt. Vernon, the mortality of parents is appreciably higher among sixth-grade children than among students in the last year of the high school. An examination of the various groups of children of high-school age not in high school shows a much higher mortality of parents here than among high-school students. In the case of young people attending the evening high school in Bridgeport, the mortality of parents is extraordinarily high, more than two and one-half times as high as among those attending the day high school. Unquestionably the disorganization of the home through the death of a parent is reflected in the diminution of the opportunities of secondary education.

While the evidence is neither quite so clear nor quite so objective, apparently the engaging in remunerative employment on the part of the mother acts in the same way as the death of a parent. Comparisons made among the groups studied usually hold in the one case as in the other. Yet, it must not be forgotten that the working mother is usually just one element in a complex social situation.

The influence of the size of the family on educational opportunity is not altogether clear. On the average, those elements in the population who do not patronize the high school have larger families than those who do, but there is no evidence to indicate that the size of the family itself is a determining factor; for the number of brothers and sisters is no smaller among Seniors than among Freshmen, and the very large families have just as high representation in the last as in the first year of the high school. Likewise the very small families do not apparently increase their representation in the later years of the high school.

The order of birth seems to be a matter of more importance, although the complexity of the situation is hardly compatible with any but the most cautious of statements. Our clearest evidence, drawn from the four groups studied in Bridgeport, indicates that the firstborn has somewhat more limited chances of securing a high-school education than the lastborn child. It is on him particularly that the burden of family support is likely to fall, if one or more of the children must help to bear it.

THE PUBLIC HIGH SCHOOL AND THE IMMIGRANT

Returns from Bridgeport and Mt. Vernon indicate very clearly that children of native parentage attend the public high school in proportionately much larger numbers than do children of immigrant parentage. There are certain immigrant groups, however, that approximate, if they do not surpass, the native stock in their zeal for secondary education, altogether apart from the social and economic handicaps under which the immigrant labors. Among these, probably the Russian Jews stand at the top, followed by the Irish, the Germans, and the peoples of the British Empire. At the other extreme are the Italians, the Poles, and the races of the old Austro-Hungarian Empire who patronize the high school in exceedingly small measure. Disregarding the record of the Russian Jews, it may be stated as a general principle that the farther east and south we go in Europe, as the source of our immigrants, we find less interest in secondary education.

The well-known tendency among our own people for the girls to patronize the high school in greater numbers than the boys is reversed among certain immigrant stocks. Thus, while in the Bridgeport High School there are but 74 boys of native parentage to every 100 girls, among the Italians this ratio of boys to girls is 154. This social trait, if such it may be called, varies much from group to group. Beginning with the Irish who exhibit the American trait in approximately its native strength of sending girls rather than boys to high school, the proportion of boys steadily increases as we pass east and south into Europe. Among the peoples of the "new" immigration the right of the girl to a secondary education is not recognized as on a parity with that of the boy.

In choice of curricula the girls of immigrant stock are clearly less inclined toward the college preparatory course than are the girls of native parentage. Curiously enough the reverse is true of the boys, but, since the boys of American parentage are exceptionally well represented in the scientific course, which in reality is a college preparatory course, no large significance should be attached to this difference between the foreign and native stock.

THE PUBLIC HIGH SCHOOL AND THE NEGRO

While for the country as a whole the proportion of negroes of high-school age to be found in our high schools is very small, in the city of St. Louis they do about as well as the whites. A study of the student population in the negro high school of this city helps us to understand the difficulties that stand in the way of educational achievement on the part of members of this race. The fathers of the students in this high school are for the most part engaged in manual labor, and the lower and less respectable grades of manual labor, particularly personal service and common labor. The negro family exhibits a large measure of disorganization, as indicated by such crude and unsatisfactory phenomena as a deceased parent or a working mother. In the high-school population of St. Louis the parental mortality for the negro children is well over twice as high as for the children of white stock, and the frequency of the working mother is between five and six times as great for the students of the one as for those of the other race. All of which makes it safe to conclude that nowhere else in the nation is there a similarly large representation of any other race living on the same social and economic level that is sending as large a proportion of its children to high school as the negroes of St. Louis.

The negroes exhibit in a pronounced fashion the American trait of sending a larger proportion of their girls than of their boys to high school. In choice of curricula, the negro girls differ from their white sisters chiefly in avoidance of the two-year commercial curriculum and in their very frequent selection of the home economics course. The negro boys avoid the general and concentrate on the manual training course. Following graduation, the negro girls expect to attend normal school and enter professional service in much larger numbers than do the whites. And they are not apparently looking forward to clerical service in proportionate numbers. Surprisingly, in the case of the boys, the only important difference between the two races is the much larger expectation of college attendance on the part of the negroes. It should be kept in mind, however, that these conclusions are based altogether on statements by the students, and consequently require considerable discounting.

THE PUBLIC HIGH SCHOOL AND PSYCHOLOGICAL SELECTION

Not only is the high-school population selected sociologically, but it is selected psychologically as well. Children of high-school age not in high school, whether they be in the evening high school, the trade school, or the continuation classes, show a lower intelligence rating on the average than do those in high school. But there is much overlapping in the distribution of ability for the two groups. There is much excellence out of, as well as much mediocrity in, the high school. The trade-school population shows a particularly wide distribution of ability.

In the high school itself the traditional academic curricula draw a higher type of ability, on the average, than do the newer and vocational curricula. Here also, however, the overlapping of the distributions is pronounced, and perhaps even more significant than the average difference.

The children from the laboring classes exhibit ability of practically as high grade as do those from the other occupational groups. This is probably due to the much greater elimination of children of labor parentage. Likewise the children of immigrants do about as well on the tests as do the children of native stock.

Firstborn make records somewhat superior to the records of lastborn children. This is probably to be explained in terms of greater elimination and thus more rigid selection among the former. The intelligence score also varies inversely with the size of the family. The explanation here is apparently to be found in the limitation of births among the more foresighted elements in the population.

THE POPULATION OF THE PRIVATE SECONDARY SCHOOL

In the population of the private secondary school, which charges a considerable tuition fee and which is fundamentally college preparatory in its function, we probably have as accurate a picture as we can get today of the sources from which the private academy drew its students before the rise of the free public high school. While this picture is certainly not accurate to the details, the general outlines in all probability do not falsify the facts.

Taking the student populations of Exeter Academy and the University of Chicago High School, we find the laboring classes practically absent, in contrast to a representation of 29 per cent in the public high school. Furthermore, these two schools draw almost three-fourths of their students from two occupational groups—the proprietors and professional service. Also almost 90 per cent of these students are of native parentage. Thus, while we may say that public secondary education is still highly selective, it is obvious that it has been and might be much more so.

CONCLUSION

Little need be said in conclusion. The story that has been told in the foregoing pages is not a new one. Misfortune, as well as fortune, passes from generation to generation. The children of unfortunate parentage are unfortunate, assuming here that the current secondary education is worth to the individual some fraction of its cost. The ancient adage, "To them that hath shall be given," is true today as in olden times. When not preserved through the operation of biological forces, the inequalities among individuals and classes are still perpetuated to a considerable degree in the social inheritance. While the establishment of the free public high school marked an extraordinary educational advance, it did not by any means equalize educational opportunity; for the cost of tuition is not the entire cost of education, or even the larger part of it. Education means leisure, and leisure is an expensive luxury. In most cases today this leisure must be guaranteed the individual by the family. Thus secondary education remains largely a matter for family initiative and concern, and reflects the inequalities of family means and ambition.

CHAPTER XVII

THE HIGH SCHOOL AND DEMOCRACY

More than twenty years ago John Dewey, in the opening paragraph of his *School and Society*, gave this expression to his conception of the ideal relation that society should sustain toward its children: "What the best and wisest parent wants for his own child, that must the community want for all of its children. Any other ideal for our schools is narrow and unlovely; acted upon, it destroys our democracy." With this ideal, properly interpreted, all believers in democracy are in sympathetic and complete accord.

At the present time, in the light of the facts revealed in this study, it is clear that we are very far from the realization of this ideal in our own country, at least in so far as secondary education is concerned. We are probably as near to it, if not somewhat nearer, than are the people of any other nation; and yet the facts do not set especially well with our professions of equality of opportunity, assuming of course that secondary education does increase an individual's chances for what we call success in modern life, as well as contribute to the general enrichment of life. In a very large measure participation in the privileges of a secondary education is contingent on social and economic status. In this connection, as in others, it would be difficult, in the thought of Bernard Shaw, to place too much emphasis on the need of a child's using wisdom in the choice of its parents; and yet, in view of the differential birthrate, the number of chances of choosing the more highly educated and well-to-do parents is distinctly limited, and is gradually becoming more so.

UNIVERSAL SECONDARY EDUCATION

But it may be maintained that this ideal of equality of educational opportunity does not mean sameness of opportunity, nor does it mean necessarily equality in years of educational experience. Some natures, as certain soils, will respond to more intensive cultivation than others. Surely no one would defend the proposition that all persons should continue their education through the three years of the university graduate school in the interests of equality of educational opportunity. The endowment of the individual must be recognized in each case. The

most that can be demanded in recognition of the ideal is that the poten-
tialities of the individual be realized. It is obvious that the selective
principle, resulting in elimination, must appear at some point in our
educational system. But at what point should the principle appear,
and under what conditions should it operate?

This really raises the question of the wisdom and justice of universal
secondary education. In theory we are apparently rather definitely
committed to the idea, although in practice we are yet very far from its
realization, as this investigation shows. If the course on which we have
embarked is unwise, it should be changed while there is time and in
the light of a thorough analysis of the matter. Should Dewey's ideal
apply to the period of secondary education? What is the place of secondary education in a democracy? Let us pass to the various considerations which these questions bring to mind.

THE FINANCIAL OBJECTION

It has been pointed out with truth that our people have embarked
upon this ambitious program of secondary education without fully
realizing the financial burden that such a program entails. The increase
in high-school enrolment has not been unattended by increasing costs.
In fact today we hear from various quarters the complaints of the tax-
payer as he is asked to meet increasingly heavy demands on his pocket-
book for educational purposes. Undoubtedly a further extension of
secondary education will mean greater educational costs. The education
of all children of high-school age would probably involve four times the
present expenditure, with no improvement in the quality of instruction.
This statement of course disregards those economies that would be
realized in the small high schools through a more intensive use of the
present teaching staff and material equipment. This would result in an
increase in the cost of secondary education to a figure somewhere between
one-half and three-quarters of a billion of dollars. And in the minds
of some people such expenditure is too stupendous to be entertained
for a moment.

A further analysis is needed, however, to discover the real nature
of this opposition to further educational expenditure. Is it that the
economic system is unable to bear the added burden; that the methods
of taxation are antiquated and not adapted to modern conditions; or
merely that the people do not regard a further extension of secondary
education as worth the cost? The first of these questions must certainly
be answered in the negative. Any nation that can spend billions on

armaments can spend a half billion on secondary education, if it so desires. A people that spends annually three billions of dollars on luxurious services, over two billions on tobacco and snuff, one billion on candy, and three-quarters of a billion on perfumery and cosmetics, need fear neither bankruptcy nor revolution by even quadrupling the present expenditure for secondary education. The economic system can bear it.

An affirmative answer to the second question can be as easily defended as the negative answer to the first. The methods of taxation for the support of education are antiquated and do not insure an equitable distribution of the burden. A century ago the property tax was fair, because property was tangible and usually a satisfactory index of an individual's ability to pay. Today the situation is quite different, due to industrialization and the increased complexity of an economic life in which property assumes many intangible forms and is no longer a fair index of ability to pay. The increase of educational costs demands, on the part of educators, close attention to the problems of taxation.

The third question is also an important and even basic one. We may at least say with assurance that, if the majority of the people want a further extension of secondary education, they will get it regardless of the cost, that is, if they want it as much or more than they want tobacco, snuff, candy, perfumery, cosmetics, and other things, for which they are spending their money now. Whether or not they want it will depend on two things: first, the value of secondary education; and second, their realization of its value. Both of these are, in large measure, problems for the educator. On the one hand, he must organize and administer secondary education in such a way and with such clarity of purpose that its value will be unequivocal and patent to the ordinary citizen without the interposition of educational sophistry and cant. Educational purpose and educational accomplishment must be stated in terms of those things that most people regard as valuable and worth while. On the other hand, the educator must inform the citizen that secondary education is so organized and so administered. Only when people are made to *feel* that education is as valuable as tobacco and cosmetics will they be as willing to spend their money for the one as for the other. But certainly the matter of cost is not in itself a sufficient reason for opposing universal secondary education.

PUBLIC SUPPORT OF SELECTIVE EDUCATION

There is another side to this question of finance that deserves attention. At the present time the public high school is attended quite

largely by the children of the more well-to-do classes.   This affords us
the spectacle of a privilege being extended at public expense to those
very classes that already occupy the privileged positions in modern
society.   The poor are contributing to provide secondary education for
the children of the rich, but are either too poor or too ignorant to avail
themselves of the opportunities which they help to provide.   But it will
be answered that the high school is supported by taxation, and that the
poor do not pay taxes.   This is obviously an unsound position to assume,
since all people who wear clothes, eat food, and live in houses do pay
taxes either directly or indirectly.   Of course, no assumption is made
here that all taxes are shifted to the consuming public, for they are not.
Some are shifted altogether, others only partially, and still others not at
all.   The consumer does pay taxes, but not the consumer only—this
and no more is assumed, but it is sufficient to warrant the foregoing
statement.

It is sometimes said in extenuation of this condition that society
as a whole profits from the education of the few through the superior
service that the few render;   and there is much that may be said in
support of this theoretical position.   In fact this is about the only
justification for public support of higher and professional education,
which are necessarily selective.   Yet in practice it must be admitted
that many individuals use the gifts of society for self-aggrandizement and
are quite unconscious of any social obligation.   This is particularly true
of education in its various forms which has been regarded too much as a
natural right or gift from God and too little as a preparation for social
service.   Indeed in many quarters it is even looked upon primarily as
a means of avoiding the hard and disagreeable work of the world and
a sure road to those callings that combine high remuneration and
respectability with the comforts of life.   Elementary education, which
is guaranteed to all, may perhaps be regarded as a natural right, but
secondary education, limited as it is, can be justified at all only in terms
of the unqualified recognition on the part of the high-school student of
the social obligation involved.   There is no such recognition in the public
high school today, although the narrow source of its students makes
this obviously and peculiarly necessary.

THE PERIL TO SOCIAL STABILITY

In some countries the universalizing of secondary education would
be viewed with alarm on the grounds that it would produce social
instability and result in the disintegration of the established order.

Indeed, such a disquieting view has been taken by some foreign educators of the effect of our limited (though extensive in comparison with other countries) secondary education on American society. The idea back of this view is apparently that it is dangerous for any society to produce a larger number of trained minds capable of self-direction and critical thought than may be required to fill the customary positions of leadership. Unquestionably there is something in this argument, if we look at it from the standpoint of those occupying the strategic and privileged positions in the existing order and who may consequently be expected to lose through any change that might be effected. On the other hand, if we are interested in the welfare of the great mass of the people, there is nothing to fear in the universalizing of secondary education; in the very considerable increase in the number of individuals capable of thoughtful leadership in every class of the population; in the presence of larger numbers of persons qualified to serve as informed and critical followers in the various social groups. In other words, any individual or any class depending on special privilege of any sort for its position in society has good reason for fearing the further extension of secondary education; all others may look upon such change with equanimity. It is of course assumed that this further extension would take into consideration all differences in individual aptitude and interest.

THE PSYCHOLOGICAL DIFFICULTY

Perhaps the strongest objection to universal secondary education is the psychological objection, to which reference has been made in an earlier paragraph. The wide range of intelligence among children of a particular age is well known, and we may assume the same for other psychological traits. Nature has thus set limits to the educability of all her children. In some this limit is very low, as in others it is extraordinarily high; at the one extreme is the idiot who can profit but little from either experience or instruction, while at the other is the child of genius for whom the most difficult intellectual tasks are easy and whose hours of instruction are very productive. To the one, secondary education is out of the question, while to the other, it is scarcely the beginning of an education that will continue throughout life.

If, however, we think less in terms of the extremes, which account for but a small proportion of the total number of cases, and more in terms of the great mass of individuals in between, much of the force of this objection is destroyed. There are undoubtedly individuals at the lower end of the distribution for whom education during the adolescent years would be unprofitable, because intellectual maturity is already practically attained, and on a very low level. Just how high the intelligence level should be in order to profit from twelve years of instruction, which takes the child through the elementary and secondary schools, is a question as yet unanswered. For certain types of subject-matter the level obviously would be higher than for others. It seems reasonable to assume that, through the proper adaptation of subject-matter and methods of instruction, secondary education might be so administered as to be profitable for all except those who are clearly feeble-minded. This would of course involve a thoroughgoing departure from the curricula and methods of the conventional type, which are the legitimate offspring of the selective principle.

That there is some scientific justification for the psychological objection to universal secondary education is admitted, but such justification does not extend to present practice. Much might be said for a secondary education that is based frankly and definitely on the principle of psychological selection, but ours is not of that type. It is true, as this study shows, that on the average, high-school students exhibit a higher intelligence level than do those children of high-school age not in high school. But what is the explanation? That the high school has purposefully selected these individuals because of their superior ability? Not at all, or at least not altogether, by any means. It seems just as probable that the selection is sociological first and psychological second; that children enter and remain in high school because they come from the homes of the influential and more fortunate classes, and not because of their greater ability. It is the usual thing for these two to go together, but a society is conceivable in which by some chance the individuals in the upper social and economic strata incline toward intellectual mediocrity. In such a society, assuming the large parental influence in determining educational opportunity which characterizes our own system, the children in high school might represent on the average a lower type of ability than those on the outside. Admitting that this is an extreme statement of the case, it nevertheless contains a certain element of truth. The high-school population includes many individuals of mediocre and inferior ability, and the population of high-school age not in high school includes many of superior talent, although the proportion on the upper levels is larger inside the high school. At the present time we have neither universal secondary education, on the one hand, nor selection according to any defensible principle, on the other.

LITTLE PLACE IN INDUSTRY FOR ADOLESCENTS

One other consideration favoring a further extension of secondary education deserves mention. In the Cleveland vocational survey it was found that there is practically no place in modern industry for children under sixteen or seventeen years of age. Normally, below this age a child enters an occupation with but little profit to either himself or society. Since there is so much that needs to be done in preparing these young people for the many and varied responsibilities of citizenship, vocation, parenthood, and the other important activities of life, and since this can hardly be accomplished in the elementary school, it seems the part of wisdom to enrich their lives and equip them to become more useful members of society through the agency of the secondary school.

A BROADER PROGRAM NECESSARY

The methods to be employed in bringing the opportunities of secondary education to practically all adolescents, regardless of class distinction, can hardly be discussed here. Undoubtedly our compulsory-education laws will have to be extended beyond the period of elementary education, and several states are already leading the way. We shall have to abandon our conventional ideas of secondary education as necessarily involving a four-year school, or a six-year school as under the reorganization, in which students attend four to six hours in the middle of the day for five days of the week during some nine or ten months of the autumn, winter, and spring seasons. Pedagogical traditions and administrative conveniences will have to adapt themselves to the conditions of life. Whether or not the community will have to go beyond the provision of free tuition and free textbooks to at least a partial support of the student during his period of attendance at school is a nice question. In certain cities where poverty and ignorance are to be found in their most extreme forms the community will probably have to bear responsibilities that the home or the individual will carry in others. But these are matters to be determined in the light of experience.

CONCLUSION

In our march toward the educational ideal referred to at the beginning of this chapter and which is clearly compatible with the professed ideals of our democracy, we must recognize two principles. *In the first place*, up to a certain point in our educational system we must have practically complete attendance of all the children of the community with adequate provision for individual differences in ability, aptitude, and interest.   Where this point should be is, in the main, an unanswered question, although there is some evidence that we shall place it well up into the secondary period and possibly at its close.   The writer is inclined to favor the latter practice, because of the tremendous educational demands of an infinitely complex world that is rapidly becoming a single society.   *In the second place,* beyond this point of complete attendance, in so far as public education is concerned, further education must rest on some objective basis rather than on the chances of circumstance and the whims of fortune.   In theory today the public supports higher education for the purpose of securing trained persons to perform those important services that require special types of ability, knowledge, skill, and discipline.   But no serious effort is made to discover the number of trained persons of each type required and the amount of training necessary in each case; nor is there a diligent search made through the lower school population for those special and superior types of ability that will most satisfactorily do those things that society wants done. Beyond the compulsory-school period a boy attends high school or college, not necessarily because of any special promise, but possibly because he is the only child of fond and well-to-do parents or because he likes football.   To be sure, we make certain minimal demands of a formal sort, but the larger purposes of this selective education are obscured, and they will remain so until they are clearly defined and their implications find definite expression in practice and tradition.   Why should we provide at public expense these advanced educational opportunities for X because his father is a banker and practically deny them to Y because his father cleans the streets of the city?   We must distinguish between that education which is for all, and that which is for the few.   At present our secondary education is of the first type in theory, and of the second in practice We must bring the theory and practice together: either open the doors of the high school to all children, and take care that all enter without favor, or frankly close its doors to all but a select group, adopt objective methods or selection, and teach to this selected group the meaning of social obligation.   There is no other course that leads to democracy, that puts the high school at the service of every class without distinction, and at the same time renders the largest service to the entire community.

INDEX

INDEX

Accuracy of returns, 12

Adolescence, secondary education as education for, 3

Adolescents, little place in industry for, 155

Age: òf fathers of high-school students, 30, 97; of mothers of high-school students, 97

Agricultural service, classification of, 22

Artisan-proprietors, classification of, 22

Austro-Hungarian Empire, 107

Austro-Hungarians: representation of, in high school, 109; ratio of boys to girls in high school among, 113

Boys to girls in high school, ratio of, 113

Bridgeport, 5, 9

British Empire, 107; representation in college preparatory course of peoples of, 111; representation in high school of peoples of, 108–9

Broader program of secondary education necessary, 155

Brothers and sisters of high-school students, number of, 102–4

Building and related trades, classification of, 23

Bureau of Education, 1, 2, 26, 114, 135

Chamber of Commerce, Seattle, 9

Chapman-Welles Test, 9, 124

Children: of high-school age, 2–3; of high-school age in high school, 2–3, 20

Children at work in Seattle, 5, 9, 46–48; mortality of parents of, 99; occupations of parents of, 46–48, 142

Children of high school age not in high school, 2–3, 5, 9, 11, 46 ff.; intelligence test records of, 125–27; mortality of parents of, 99–100; occupations of parents of, 52–54, 142

Chinese in Seattle, 16

Cities studied, the four, 14 ff.; geographical location of, 14; history of, 15–16; industries of, 18; occupations of people of, 17–18; property in, value of, 18; proportion of children in high school in, 20; racial and ethnic composition of people of, 16–17

Classification of occupations, 21–25

Clerical service, classification of, 22

Commercial service, classification of, 22

Common labor, classification of, 23

Comparison: of high-school population and adult population, 28 ff.; of high-school Seniors and adult population, 42–43; of sixth grade and Senior year of high school, 41–42

Compulsory continuation classes of Bridgeport, 6, 11; intelligence test records of children in, 125–27; mortality of parents of children in, 99–100; occupations of parents of children in, 51–52

Course of study and parental occupation, 55 ff.; of high-school students in Bridgeport, 55–58; of high-school students in Mt. Vernon, 58–62; of high-school students in St. Louis, 62–68; of high-school students in Seattle, 68–72

Cultural level and educational opportunity, 87 ff.

Democracy and the high school, 149 ff.

Democratization of secondary education, 140

Denmark, 107

Dewey, John, 149

Elementary-school enrolment, 1, 2

Equality of educational opportunity, 149

Evening high school of Bridgeport, 6, 11; intelligence test records of students in, 125–27; mortality of parents of students in, 99–100; occupations of parents of students in, 48–50

Exceptions to method of procedure, 8–9

Expectations: of boys following graduation, 81 ff.; of girls following graduation, 75 ff.; following graduation, and parental occupation, 74 ff.

Family: size of, and educational opportunity, 102–4; influences and high-school attendance, 94 ff., 144

Fathers: of high-school students, age of, 30; of high-school students, mortality of, 96